IMAGES
of America

WILDOMAR

IMAGES
of America

WILDOMAR

Robert Cashman

ARCADIA
PUBLISHING

Published by Arcadia Publishing
Charleston SC, Chicago IL, Portsmouth NH, San Francisco CA

Library of Congress Control Number: 2009924706

For all general information contact Arcadia Publishing at:
Telephone 843-853-2070
Fax 843-853-0044
E-mail sales@arcadiapublishing.com
For customer service and orders:
Toll-Free 1-888-313-2665

Visit us on the Internet at www.arcadiapublishing.com

This book is dedicated to the families and individuals that have made Wildomar their home in the past and to those who still live here and make Wildomar what it is today. It is my hope that this book may provide enjoyment and benefit to future generations. A special dedication goes to my own family—my wife, Diane, and our five children, Crystal, Kimberly, Beth, Jennifer, and Robert.

CONTENTS

ACKNOWLEDGMENTS

Little has been gathered in one place about the unique story of Wildomar and its people, so that story is told in this book. We have to thank the board of the Wildomar Historical Society: Edy Rodarme, Kathe Sabetzadeh, Sharon Heil, Richard Heil, Vicki Long, Nancy Noble, and George Cambero for helping to gather and organize the photographs. We have also appreciated the assistance of the Arcadia publishing staff, particularly Debbie Seracini. All images used in this book came from the Wildomar Historical Society archives unless otherwise noted. The photographs in the initial part of the book concerning Wildomar's early days were compiled by David A Brown.

The Wildomar Historical Society is especially appreciative of the response and interest of the following persons who donated or shared their pictures and stories: David Turner, Nancy Jane Brown, Mary Wilks Gatch, Philip Mobley, Geraldine Pelletier Moncour, Michel Thomas, Susan Morgan, Herman DeJong, Rose and Lee Tompkins, Judy Tompkins Kathriner, Tom and Anne Wilks, E. Hale Curran, Stan Smith, Mary and Joe Ortega, Rich and Sue Skinner, Mary Ellen Robbins, Sydney Van Loon, Mary Diane Simmons, Beth Taylor, Ruth Adkins, Gloria Smith, Rick and Sue Skinner, Gerry Stevenson, Merv and Marlene Messaros, Charles G. Tunstall, Kathy Pierce, Alex Sukhov, Vladimir Sukhov, Joseph Zakour, Jean Hayman, Robert Ambler, Cal Taylor, Dorothy Taylor, Phil Taylor, Jon Neal, Vicki and Larry Long, Dorothy Davis, John, Joe, and Anthony Cantacessi, Denise Sewell, Diana Autumn and Anne Sullivan Nursery School, Lakeview Chapel, Wildomar Chamber of Commerce, Keith Herron, and the Riverside County Parks and Open Space District.

The captions under the photographs acknowledge other residents who are part of the historical aspects of the book. Acknowledgment is also given to Elizabeth Pomeroy and Many Moons Press for a quote from the book *Sage Bloom and Water Rights: Stories of Early Southern California*, a collection of Margaret Collier Graham's stories. Finally, acknowledgment is given to Robert Austin for his permission to quote a selection from a poem by Cranston Stroup from the collection of poems *Give God a Flower* published by Creekside Press.

INTRODUCTION

Wildomar had an auspicious beginning, since it was a community that was planned and structured in 1885 by its three founders to provide all of the necessities that towns at the time required. With the stagecoach, railroad, and then Highway 395 winding through the area, the town was poised for success. It cannot be said that the story of Wildomar is the story of any one particular family. Rather let it be noted that it is the story over time of the many families that lived here and of their connection to the land itself; the hills, the arroyos, the springs, and the agricultural interests.

"The story of Wildomar cannot be told without relating how three men, with confidence in the future of Southern California, purchased the Rancho La Laguna and started the colony of Elsinore." So starts the year 1883 in a historical paper as told by Iva Keegan, the well-known teacher at Wildomar School from 1928 to 1948. It was two short years later in 1885 that the copartnership of the three men—Graham, Collier, and Heald—was dissolved, and the land was divided between the men. Heald took the Elsinore portion.

Donald Graham and William Collier took the portion that was southwesterly to Corydon Road, about 2,500 acres. Margaret Collier Graham, the sister of William Collier and the wife of Donald Graham, coined the name of Wildomar for this land from the first syllables of the first names of the three founders, WILliam Collier, DOnald Graham, and MARgaret Collier Graham. Wildomar was born!

With the connection of the Southern Pacific Railroad through Wildomar in 1885, the stage was set for a western migration from the Midwestern states. Wildomar was established by its founders as a colony. The townsite was laid out, and essential functions were established. The year of 1886 saw the establishment of the Wildomar Post Office, the Wildomar School, a train station, two churches, and water piped in the streets. The Wildomar Hotel was financed by Collier and Graham to house the prospective settlers from Kansas, Iowa, Indiana, and surrounding states. Ranches, a few general stores, a livery, and a blacksmith shop rounded out the community.

Wildomar was promoted as a place to settle and call your home. In the words of William Collier, "With $2,000 you can buy 5 acres of land at Wildomar, plant it with trees, build a house that will make a small family comfortable, dig a well and put up a windmill and have something left to buy other necessaries." Stories about many of Wildomar's significant people, places, and buildings are found in the pages of this book. Pioneers included the Wilks, Torbett, Catt, McVicar, and Brown families, among others.

The settlement of the community saw the gradual replacement of stagecoaches and horse-and-buggies with the automobile. Most travel was already being done with a system of roads, chief of which was Highway 395. The highway became a major north-south part of the California state highway system. By 1920, this highway was mostly complete. Gas stations and restaurants were located on Palomar Street (then called Highway 395) serving the growing auto traffic. Until around 1928 there was still a regular stagecoach that went to Riverside. Unfortunately for the area, the railroad line to San Diego was discontinued after the tracks were washed out and not replaced. Temecula became the end of the line. In 1935, the last train ran through Wildomar and the tracks were torn up. Another important event in the area was the 1952 rerouting of Highway 395. Renamed Highway 71, it bypassed the Palomar Road and Mission Trail connection that went through the downtown area. This considerably impacted the businesses along the route and decreased their economic health.

Throughout its history agriculture has been important to Wildomar. Honey production was an important business; boxcar loads of honey were produced in the area as early as 1911. In 1967, a large honey factory was operating off of Central Avenue providing honey to Sue Bee. Until the early 1980s, sheep that were driven to pastures were sometimes seen blocking the dirt roads. Other industries of importance over the years were apricots, concord grapes, cattle, turkey and rabbit meat, and a dairy. In the early 1900s, olives were important, with an olive cannery located in Lakeland Village where some olive oil was also produced. This is the reason for the 1,000 or so olive trees that are scattered throughout Wildomar and neighboring Lakeland Village.

In the 1930s and 1940s, there was a drought, and some of the farmers dug deeper wells and increased their production of alfalfa and row crops. Fruit and nut orchards decreased in importance. With the ready availability of grain and hay, cattle and sheep became prominent. As late as 1969, there were 1,400 acres being planted and harvested by David A. Brown. DeJong's Dairy, which had been originally located near Wildomar School, moved in 1961 to its current location south of Corydon Road.

With the replacement of Highway 71 (a winding two lane road from Corona to San Diego) by the I-15 freeway around 1985, the community of Sedco/Sedco Hills was broken up. The new freeway transected the center of town and separated the community into two sections. This entire area later became part of the city of Wildomar. Along the neighboring Central/Baxter area, the stage was set for housing tracts and rapid development. The neighboring cities of Murrieta, Temecula, and Lake Elsinore were on the fast track to change. However, Wildomar developed slowly and today is still a mix of larger properties, rural areas, and an urbanized area with shopping centers.

In terms of its development, there were five major waves of settlers: the 1880s that brought the pioneers and speculators; the 1920s with settlers that were farm oriented with dryland farming predominating; the 1940s–1950s with settlers seeking a more rural alternative to the metropolitan areas; the 1970s with the coexistence of horse ranches and the first housing tracts; and after 1982, a wave of commuters found haven in Wildomar as the neighboring cities became built out.

The desire for Wildomar to remain independent and create its own destiny was strong in the community. The Wildomar Incorporation Now (WIN) spearheaded the incorporation effort. There were many obstacles, as both the State of California and Riverside County's Local Agency Formation Commission (LAFCO) made cityhood a strenuous and difficult task. Finally, on February 4, 2008, the issue went to a vote. The people of Wildomar voted to become a city.

On July 1, 2008, the city of Wildomar was born amidst fireworks and celebration. It is expected that the small-town atmosphere, the community spirit, and family-centered environment will remain essential aspects of the community.

One

PIONEERS AND SPECULATORS

There is a theory that Wildomar's initial existence is owed to three historical factors: the settling of the American West, the price war between the railroads, and the Krakatoa volcanic eruption in the Pacific Ocean in 1883.

Since 1846, Southern California had been in a long, cyclic drought and the neighboring La Laguna Lake (Lake Elsinore) was virtually dry. Suddenly, with the heavy rains (65 inches) in the first three months of 1884, the lake was filled to the brim. Numerous springs and a high water table made orchards and farms seem particularly attractive. Wildlife teemed in the surrounding area. Wildomar must have looked like the land of opportunity to the first settlers in 1887. There is speculation that the rain that made this possible was due to the volcanic explosion at Krakatoa.

Wildomar was part of the general migration of settlers from the Eastern states to the West, in particular from the Midwest states. The local Native Americans were not an aspect of the growing community, having been driven from their lands and relocated in 1875 by the U.S. cavalry. Evidence of their earlier settlement is found in the numerous grinding bowls and manos discovered in Wildomar.

In 1886, William Collier and Donald Graham, who owned Wildomar, platted the city and its town center and marketed it to their friends and relatives back home. It was their good fortune that travel by rail suddenly became inexpensive as two competing railroads vied for business. Unfortunately, within a year, speculators drove land prices all throughout San Diego County to levels that could not be maintained. The 1888 collapse followed. Vaguely reminiscent of the current housing situation, many people lost money as their houses and properties were foreclosed.

To their credit and to our benefit, the founders and their families stayed around to develop and promote the two cities they established, Wildomar and South Pasadena. Fortunately, the railroad connected both cities, allowing the families to travel back and forth between their two locations. William Collier returned to live in Wildomar full time in later years.

All three of the Wildomar founders came from the Midwest. Around 1871, Donald Graham married Margaret Collier and lived in Bloomington, Illinois, until Donald's health deteriorated, forcing him to look for a better climate. Donald M. Graham, the son of a preacher, graduated in 1869 from Monmouth College in Monmouth, Illinois, along with classmates Margaret and Jennie E. Collier and their brother William. The weather in Southern California was drier and his health improved, even though tuberculosis was to follow him all his life until his untimely death at age 43. Donald became interested in real estate and purchased land in Pasadena, planting it with orange trees. It was at that time that he went into a venture with Frank Heald to purchase Rancho La Laguna. For reasons that were never clear, the partnership dissolved and the two later split the land, with the Wildomar portion south of Corydon Road becoming the property of the Colliers and the Grahams. (Courtesy Huntington Library.)

William Collier and his wife, Ella, moved from Keokuk Iowa to California in late 1884, making his first home in San Diego to facilitate, at the county level, legal matters pertaining to the subdivisions of Rancho La Laguna. In 1885, the La Laguna partnership with Frank Heald broke up and Margaret Collier Graham coined the name for Wildomar from the first letter of the names William, Donald, and Margaret. In 1885, the community was surveyed and platted. On April 16, 1886, the Wildomar Post Office was established. In 1887, the Wildomar Hotel and Presbyterian church was built. William Collier had a law practice in Riverside and traveled frequently back and forth between Wildomar and Riverside. In 1914, he retired and spent the rest of his days living on Central Avenue in Wildomar. (Courtesy Riverside County Library.)

Margaret Collier Graham and her sister Jennie Collier travelled to California with her seriously ill husband, Donald Graham, carried on a stretcher. The climate in California was said to have healing power, and his health improved for a short time. After Donald's death at age 43, Margaret settled in South Pasadena but continued the administration of the Graham properties in Wildomar and the Alberhill Coal Company with the aid of her sister Jennie. Margaret earned a living by writing and making appearances on the lecture circuit. She was a vocal supporter of women's rights and was a suffragette. *Stories of the Foot-hills* (1895) and *The Wizard's Daughter* (1905) were two collections of her stories. The *Land of Sunshine* carried her column, in which she discussed manners, morals, the woman's point of view, the value of willpower, the pursuit of happiness, and the necessity of good taste. (Courtesy USC Libraries.)

SAN DIEGO COUNTY

SOUTHERN

CALIFORNIA

A SEMI-TROPIC PARADISE

PRESENTED BY THE

WILDOMAR

LAND AND WATER COMPANY

Wildomar, Cal.

See Pages 46, 47 and 48

The county of San Diego stretched from the Arizona border to the Pacific Ocean. According to an article in the *Warner Brothers Annual*, "Bargains in Real Estate will be shown which will challenge the past, present, and future for equals. Wildomar claims to be unrivaled in bright prospects. We will prove correct all of our statements. Not a promise has ever been made for Wildomar that has not been performed. Not a prediction that has not been fulfilled". The same publication had advertisements from various banks with "money to loan in large and small amounts."

13

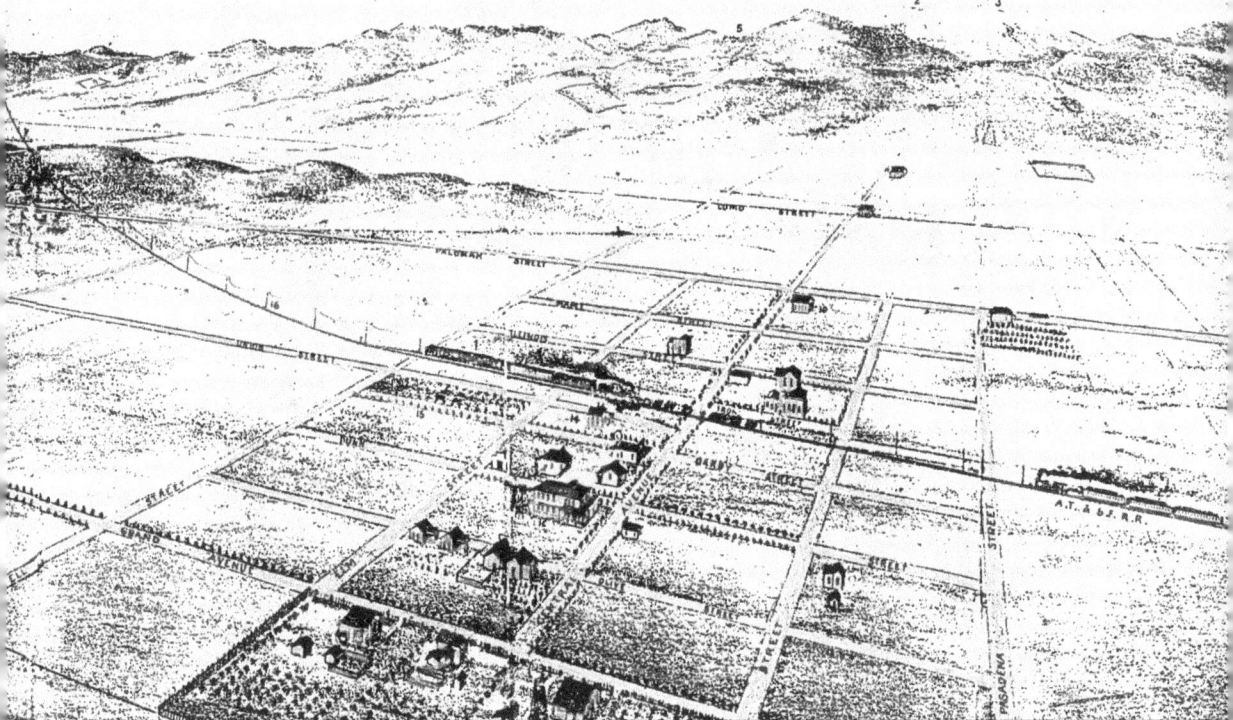

The center portion of the 1887 prospectus prepared by William Collier and Donald Graham to entice people to move shows a train coming from both directions on the same track. The brochure states, "Wildomar claims its full share of advantages. Our climate, scenery, soil, water facilities, post office, railroad station, hotel, store, and other business houseer and last, and perhaps most, our prosperous fruit and stock farms make us *faciie princeps*. Our location on the main line of the great A.T. and S.F.R.R. [Atchison, Topeka, and Santa Fe Railway] from Boston to San Diego, is an advantage. Our population of industrious well-to-do people is our pride and our guarantee for the future." The flood of people who came included those industrious families described in the brochure. Along with them came real estate speculators who drove the land prices higher and higher until there was an inevitable real estate crash. (Courtesy Alida Pearson.)

This combination store and post office was featured in a promotional advertisement by William Collier in 1887. It was also featured in an E. Embree and Company advertisement the same year. Clint Lewis bought the building in September 9, 1887. (Courtesy Robert Ambler.)

This is another view of the original post office building, which continued in use at this location until it was moved by postmaster Fred Orvis around 1927 to Palomar Street opposite Wildomar School. John Rodriquez, the new owner, demolished the building in April 1957. Note the mail letter slot to the left of the left window and A. L. Matthew against the post on the right side of the photograph. (Courtesy Robert Ambler.)

The Hotel Wildomar had its grand opening on May 13, 1887. Soon thereafter it housed many visitors from the Midwest who were looking to buy a farm. The hotel was located southwest of Dunn Street and northwest of Central Avenue. It was the scene of many social events. During the Great Depression, Clint Lewis planned to move it to Riverside. It is believed that the hotel burned down before it could be moved. (Courtesy E. Hale Curran.)

Mr. Sam C. Pearson + Ladies

The pleasure of your presence is requested at the Opening of the

Hotel Wildomar.

Thursday Evening, May 12th, 1887.

D. M. Graham.   Wm. Collier.
              E. E. Wilson.

For important affairs, formal invitations were the norm, even in a new town. E. E. Wilson was the proprietor of the hotel. The hotel was described in the brochure as a "substantial and comfortable hotel with 20 rooms open for the accommodation of guests." (Courtesy David Turner.)

The United Presbyterian Church was dedicated on Thanksgiving Day 1888. Reverend Jamison was the pastor. The high peaked roof and steeple show that the builders were from a place in the Midwest or the East where heavy snows would fall. The church was located on Central Street. (Courtesy E. Hale Curran.)

Standing in front of Wildomar School on a Sunday afternoon (about 1914), parishioners have their picture taken dressed in their Sunday best. The Presbyterian church was located on the other side of Central Street near the Wildomar School. (Courtesy E. Hale Curran.)

This is a 1918 view of the United Presbyterian Church. Rudolph Brown and his children, David, Wilfred, Jerry, and Kathleen, attended this church during the 1920s through the 1930s. The church was torn down in 1942. As was typical of the time, the lumber was salvaged. It was used to build the Sharer Hall, an addition to the Methodist church in Murrieta. (Courtesy David A. Brown.)

The Embree and Pearson families pose for this 1891 photograph. Ezra Embree was the Wildomar postmaster and storekeeper in 1887. Pictured here are, from left to right, (first row) Elizabeth Pearson, Bessie Embree, A. Alida Pearson, and George Embree; (second row) David and Annie Michener Pearson (Wildomar residents 1886–1893) and Samuel Pearson; (third row) William Embree, Virginia Pearson Embree, Charles Pearson, and George Pearson. (Courtesy Robert Ambler.)

The Pearson home was located southwest of Grand Avenue and west of Gruwell Street. The house was built in the vernacular style with Victorian adornment and is believed to have also been the home of John Belk and his wife during the 1930s. (Courtesy Robert Ambler.)

This is the 1892 survey book of George M. Pearson created for the Santa Rosa Ranch addition to Wildomar in 1892. George M. Pearson, who had been employed in the engineering of the Wildomar irrigation system that is based on wells, became Riverside County's first county surveyor. Riverside County was created in 1893 out of San Diego County whose county seat was San Diego, which became difficult to reach after the 1892 flood in Temecula canyon. (Courtesy David A. Brown.)

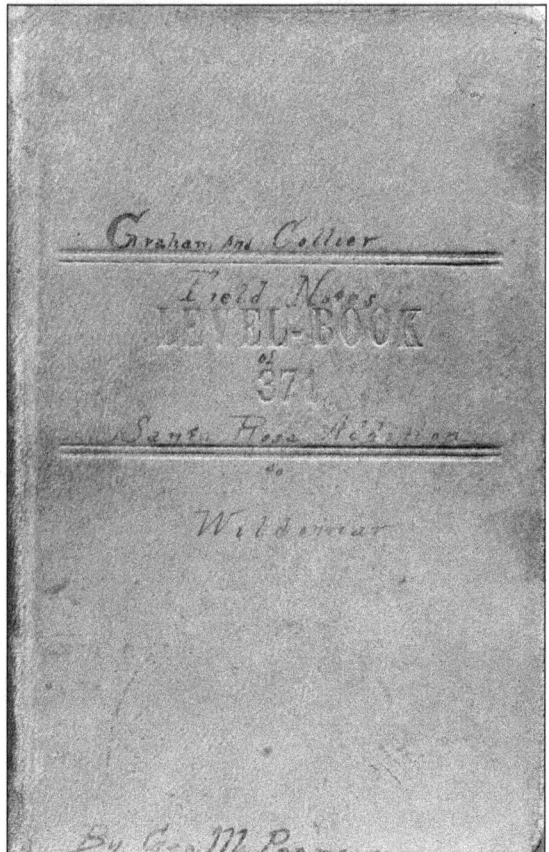

Four generations of the Browns pose in 1916 at Dr. Oscar Brown's second home at 1263 West Tenth Street in Riverside. Pictured from left to right are Columbus Brown, father of Dr. Oscar S. Brown (1826–1917); Rudolph Brown, son of Dr. Oscar S. Brown (1891–1970); and Dr. Oscar S. Brown (1858–1949). The baby is Wilfred Oscar Brown (1915–1968). (Courtesy David A. Brown.)

Standing in front of the Wildomar home of Oscar Brown in 1902 are, from left to right, Columbus Brown, father of Dr. Oscar Brown and later a Wildomar School District school board trustee; Dr. Oscar Samuel Brown; his daughter, Prudence; his wife, Verona C. Brown; and an unidentified woman. The home is located near the southern corner of Elm and Olive Streets, now known as Pecan Street. (Courtesy David A. Brown.)

This rustic cabin was located in Wildomar. Note the roughly finished tree trunk used as a post for the roof of the porch. Since the other side has the same feature, this is likely to have been a design element. (Courtesy David A. Brown.)

The Colliers and Grahams are at a picnic in 1884 on the Elsinore Lake. According to the inscription on the back, pictured from left to right are (first row) Alice Collier, Helen Collier, Ella J. Collier; (second row) Margaret Collier Graham, Donald M. Graham, Wm Collier, and Jennie E. Collier. The photographer's wife is standing down by the shore. (Courtesy David Turner).

The Ben F. Taylor home was located on the southwest corner of Dunn and Gruwell Streets. The wood for the house was ordered precut from a catalogue and shipped by rail to Wildomar. Water came from a windmill into the kitchen sink. The building is seen during the snowstorm in late December 1915–January 1916. According to the written records of William Collier, about 10 inches of snow fell during that time. (Courtesy Robert Ambler.)

Mary Soules, mother of Fanny Taylor, is standing in front of B. F. Taylor's bedroom window in 1916 with her daughter's children, Jim Taylor (about six years old) and Ellen Taylor (about three years old). Fanny came from Michigan to study to be a teacher at the Normal School in Whittier. She came to Wildomar to teach at Wildomar Elementary in 1906 and married B. F. Taylor in 1907. (Courtesy John C. Taylor.)

The home of Mary Soules was located on the southeast side of Darby Street on the second lot from Central Street in 1916. From 1938 to 1946, this was the home of Frank Taylor and Dorothy (Rail) Taylor. The house was the birthplace of Calvin and Philip Taylor. (Courtesy John C. Taylor.)

The Ben Taylor house was built in 1914 and 1915. Located at 21343 Dunn Street, it was still in excellent condition in 1981. The porch (veranda) has two entry doors, and battened porch piers with similar shiplap siding. (Courtesy Riverside Park and Open Space District.)

In 1891, the view of Wildomar from the hills to the west of the town looked like this. To the right, a thick row of trees lined Central Street. The community warehouse in the center marks where the Southern California Railroad passed through. Grand Avenue is visible through the trees in the foreground. The white tower of the Methodist Episcopal Church is visible beyond the warehouse at Palomar and Central Streets. (Courtesy David A. Brown.)

By 1924, the first park in Wildomar benefited from the many shade trees that had been planted in the early part of the century. The park was located between Elm and Gruwell Streets and west of Darby. The park was later abandoned, and in the 1930s the land reverted to the original owners, the Colliers. (Courtesy David A. Brown.)

The first post office opened in Wildomar in August 1886 with Isaac Penrose as postmaster. The post office was the house of Isaac Penrose barely seen in the left of the photograph near Central Avenue. The settlers planted trees along the main streets in Wildomar. In the photograph, Central Street is seen around 1931, looking from Grand Avenue toward Palomar Street. (Courtesy David A. Brown.)

Local residents are enjoying a ride in Wildomar around 1914. From left to right are Everly Davis, H. C. Fletcher, Mary Simmons, and an unidentified woman and child. Mary Simmons married Dean Fletcher. Dean and Mary moved to their home at the west corner of Grand Avenue and Central Street. (Courtesy Ellen Taylor Hazard.)

This house at 32785 Central Street was built in 1885 by William Collier, one of Wildomar's founders. Photographed in 1981, the house appears to be in good condition. The house has redwood clapboard siding, two front doors, double hung windows, and a shed-roofed porch. Between 1915 and 1920, William Collier added a library room to the house, which served as the first library in Wildomar. (Courtesy Riverside Park and Open Space District.)

Built sometime between 1886 and 1899 for W. G. McVicar, this is his one-and-a-half-story vernacular ranch house at 22180 Grand Avenue that has redwood ship lath siding. W. G. McVicar, a lumber dealer in Corona, became a major investor in Wildomar and the first Riverside County supervisor from the first supervisorial district. In this 1981 photograph, two bathtubs serve as planters. (Courtesy Riverside Park and Open Space District.)

The substantial two-story houses in Wildomar showed that the residents intended to stay. Resting under the trees in front of their house in 1898 are Mr. and Mrs. Abram Matthews. (Courtesy David Turner.)

The two thick rock walls in a hillside, facing each other, flank an entrance to the Iodine Springs in Wildomar. Constructed around 1925 by the original owners of the Iodine Springs Resort—Mr. and Mrs. Curtiss, also the owners of Curtiss Candy Company—it supplied water for the cabins, tents, and swimming pool. The waters from this spring were said to have medicinal qualities and were bottled and sold. (Courtesy Riverside Park and Open Space District.)

GRANT DEED

Mrs G.F.DeLany

to

Verona C Brown

Dated _____ 7/8/99

Received For Record

OCT 16 1889

at 46 min. past 10 o'clock A.M. at
request of Consolidated Bank
Copied in Book No. 8H of
Deeds page 215 et
seq., Records of Riverside County,
California.

E H Gruwell Recorder.

By _____
Deputy Recorder

Fees, $ .00

FOR SALE BY
PUTNAM FIELD
Printer
Lawyers Block, San Diego, Cal.

#15655

CERTIFICATE
—OF—
TITLE
—TO—

Por. Lot 5, Block "K",
Elsinore.

TELEPHONE MAIN 47.   COMPLETE
Properly Index   RAYMOND BEST MANAGER.

The Riverside
ABSTRACT CO.
Certificates of Title a specialty.
EXACT INFORMATION FURNISHED.
RIVERSIDE, CAL.

Buying and selling land was a second occupation for many farmers. On the left is a deed for a property on October 16, 1889, that is recorded to Verona Brown, the wife of Rudolph Brown. E. H. Gruwell, who gave his name to Gruwell Street in Wildomar, records the deed. On the right is a "certificate of title" also for Verona Brown. (Courtesy Robert Cashman.)

Two

DRYLAND FARMING

Among the 100 or so family farms around the area in 1890, two farmers—Dr. Oscar Brown and Tom Wilks—and their families maintained a continuous presence in Wildomar from the 1880s to recent times. Both specialized in dryland farming with some other farming jobs to supplement their income. These jobs included: small fruit and nut orchards, collecting and selling honey, cattle, and miscellaneous work such as drilling wells. Buying and selling land rounded out the finances.

Dr. Oscar Brown, a physician and surgeon for the Santa Fe Railroad, settled in Wildomar in 1897. The Brown properties were farmed by his son Rudolph Brown, and later by David A. Brown, his grandson. The original acreage was increased by purchase and leasing, and by 1955 they were planting and harvesting about 1,200 acres. In that year, 100 acres of Chilean variety alfalfa were planted for seed, and 600 acres of grain were planted for wheat, oats, or hay. The remainder of the land lay fallow. Rudolph Brown was a scientific farmer, having graduated from Berkeley with a degree in agriculture. He, and later his son David, continued the rainfall record book and weather record started in 1913 by William Collier. The exact timing of planting in dryland farming makes a difference between profit and loss for the year.

Tom Wilks, the "alfalfa king", lived about a half mile from the Browns. The Wilks property contained a spring that fed a pool that had been a watering place for the horses of the Butterfield Stage. His children all attended Wildomar School along with the other families in the area. Like all of the pioneer families, he participated in the active life of the community.

Ben Taylor came to Wildomar in 1906 to become a dryland farmer and then operated a turkey ranch for 50 years. The Freeman, Torbett, and Cantacessi families are among other long established Wildomarians.

Rudolph Brown's crew is seen threshing wheat in the Wildomar area around 1930 near the present-day Bear Creek Golf course. David Brown, about 12 years old at the time, is in the left rear of the photograph. Also featured are Willard Letner, mule skinner, and Wilfred Brown, header tender. Rudolph Brown, sack sewer, is taking the picture and not shown. (Courtesy David A. Brown.)

Rudolph Brown's crew is hauling sacks of wheat to his ranch in Wildomar after the threshing is completed for the day on the Vail Company Cole Canyon lease area in Wildomar in summer 1930. The harvesting was normally done from July to September and was hot, dusty work. (Courtesy David A. Brown).

Rudolph Brown's threshing crew in 1930 is at work near the present-day Bear Creek Golf Course. Willard Letner was the mule skinner, Wilfred Brown was the head tender, and David Brown was the brakeman, side hill leveler, and sack sewer. This was quite a job for a 12-year-old. The only relief from the heat was the shade from the roof and the valley breeze. (Courtesy David A. Brown.)

David Brown is plowing around the Baxter Road area in 1949 in Wildomar. This is the first plow to use hydraulic lift and depth control. The control was invented by Rudolph Brown and Harry Schroeder in about 1941. (Courtesy David A. Brown.)

The poet Cranston Stroup worked for Rudolph Brown as a ranch hand in Wildomar for two summers in the 1930s. In the book *Give God a Flower* by Creekside Press, he reflects on the tension between natural beauty and agricultural productivity. In *Caterpillar 60*, Cranston writes the following:

> But I drop the ploughs, and set the gears in low for the long, slow pull of slope. The plow cuts deep . . . the ribbons turn as 60 horses strain the bar. The flowers sink to graves of unmarked beauty . . . and so, ten thousand to a furrow, bits of sky, and tiny fragments of the sun are buried under shrouds of quiet earth.

In this photograph, the 10-foot wheat field plow is ready for action in 1940 on the Rudolph Brown ranch. The wheels on the plow are metal to dig into the ground during plowing. Assorted farm tools, including a mower, are in the background. (Courtesy David A. Brown.)

Jerry Brown and his dog, Skip, pose in 1940 beside a farmer's friend, the D-6 Caterpillar tractor. The tractor was used for planting, tilling, and harvesting on Rudolph Brown's 600-acre farm. It could easily pull 30 feet of grain drill in seeding barley or wheat. The drills would put the seed in the soil fairly deep, at least an inch, to discourage the birds from feeding on the seeds. Planting time usually started with the first November rains. (Courtesy David A. Brown.)

A thresher is being pulled by a tractor on a Wildomar hillside. The umbrella was the earlier-day analogue of the enclosed cabin and air-conditioning present in today's equipment. The weight of the tractor and its low center of gravity compensate for the unbalanced position of the thresher. (Courtesy David A. Brown.)

David Brown and his brother Jerry were expected and required to help their father, Rudolph, run the farm. Jerry Brown is ready to work using a sickle mower in 1940. The sickle mower was a very useful implement, as it could be used either with tractors or with mules or horses, depending on the front attachment. (Courtesy David A. Brown.)

A combine harvester pulled by 12 mules is pictured around 1930. Off to the right is the five-story hay barn on the Rudolph Brown property. A pulley was used to lift the hay into the loft. Up to 1,500 acres of land would be planted and harvested each season. (Courtesy David A. Brown.)

This is the famous five-story hay barn of Rudolph J. Brown on his property at 22060 Grand Avenue. Built in 1886, it is seen here in September 1981. The concave gable roof of redwood shingles is partially covered with corrugated sheet metal. The building has vertical redwood plank siding and includes a loft opening with a beam for hauling up bales of hay. (Courtesy Riverside Park and Open Space District.)

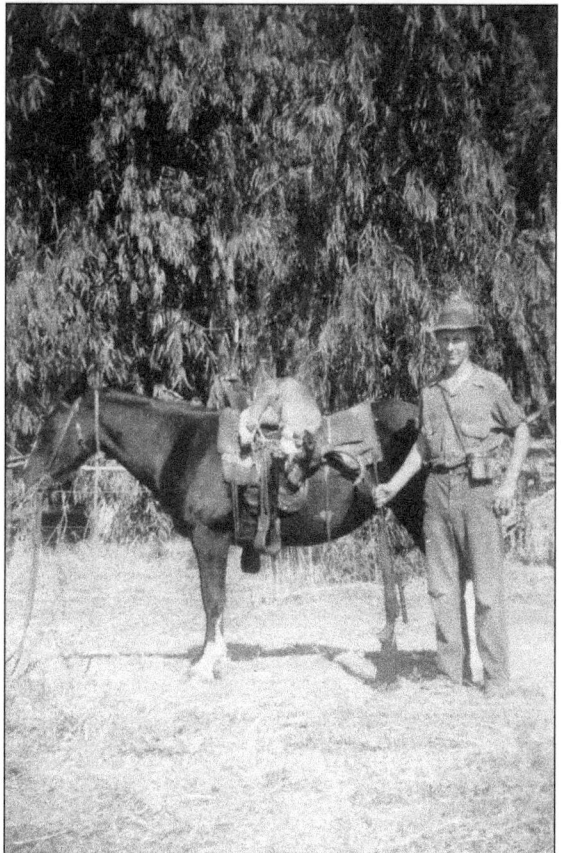

The mountains around Wildomar in 1940 teemed with deer, badgers, bobcats, and other wildlife. Hunting was a favorite sport for many of the pioneering families. Jerry Brown was successful in bagging his deer and transporting him by horse back to the ranch. (Courtesy David A. Brown.)

Jerry Brown and his faithful companion go hunting in the hills near the ranch. Rabbits, dove, and quail were sometimes hunted for meals, even breakfast. The rifle was also used for rattlesnakes. Like many pioneering families, the front room of the Brown family house had a mantle that featured the skin of a bobcat. (Courtesy David A. Brown.)

A granite wall with stone from the Wildomar quarry in the 1880s is at the base of the front side of the Rudolph Brown ranch house. The screened in front porch in this 1980 photograph was later walled in, and a second set of windows was added. To the left of the house is the water tower that supplied water for the horses and cattle. (Courtesy Riverside Park and Open Space District.)

This is the back view of the Rudolph Brown water tower and ranch house, as seen in 1940. The entrance to the underground cellar is located on the left side of the house in the photograph. The cellar was probably dug in the 1930s. The walls were cemented by nailing chicken wire to the dirt walls and laying concrete over the wire. (Courtesy David A. Brown.)

On Christmas Day 2001, the Rudolph Brown house, the garage, 1930s barn buildings, and a radio tower structure were all still intact but unfortunately were in the path of development. A last-minute deal with the developer saved the house and the water tower, but all the other structures were destroyed. The eucalyptus trees were 170 feet tall and were cut for firewood. (Courtesy Robert Cashman.)

The Rudolph Brown house and tower (in two pieces) were moved across the dirt field adjacent to the house, down McVicar Street, along Palomar Road and right on Central Street to be temporarily positioned on Baxter Road near the freeway. Younger Brothers moved both structures between 12:00 a.m. and 5:00 a.m. on the morning of January 1, 2006. (Courtesy Robert Cashman.)

David A. Brown was born on September 15, 1918. Like his father, Rudolph Brown, Dave was a farmer and rancher on the land in and around Wildomar all his life. He died on August 18, 1993. A tireless promoter of Wildomar and its history, he was involved in the creation of the Wildomar Interest League and was the Zone 7 flood commissioner. The words "Mr. Wildomar" are engraved on his grave marker. (Courtesy Nancy Jane Brown.)

When David Brown needed a place for his amateur radio headquarters, he put a station in the former chicken shed and constructed this UF antenna. As a member of the Lake Elsinore Valley Amateur Radio Club, he was part of the emergency preparedness organization at the time. Dave was a member of the Volunteers in Prevention (VIP) Amateur Radio Program that provided communications for the California Department of Forestry. (Courtesy Nancy Jane Brown.)

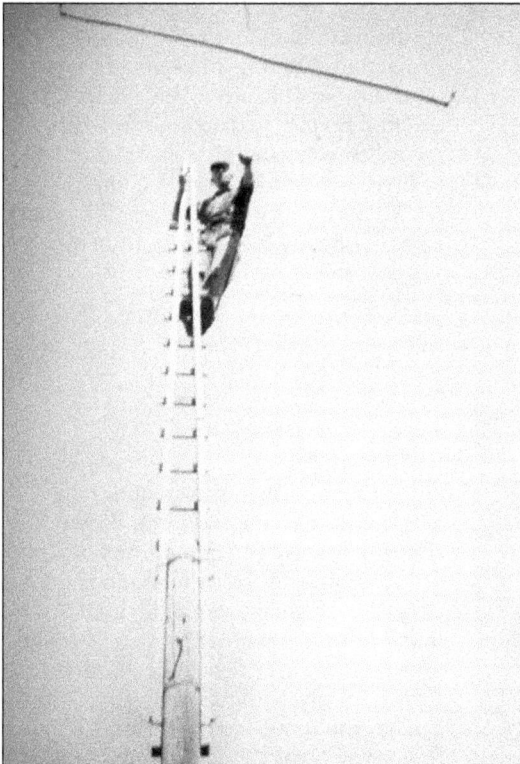

David Brown adjusts the orientation of the antenna. The office of disaster preparedness in Riverside issued him a civil defense identification card. Dave was a member of the Radio Amateur Civil Emergency Services (RACES)—call letters W6NBM, county warning and forecast Area. (Courtesy Nancy Jane Brown.)

David Brown shows the rainfall measuring instruments first used by William Collier, later by Rudolph Brown, and then by himself. The book on the table in front of Dave is the original bound volume used by Collier to record the weather on a daily basis. One of Dave's great loves was Wildomar. He felt he had a duty to preserve Wildomar's past. (Courtesy Nancy Jane Brown.)

Nancy Jane Brown, shown at age 25, was the woman behind Dave Brown. She was involved in community activities and active at Wildomar School with their son David. Like many other pioneering women, she was an essential part of the success of the Brown family. Still mentally active at age 88, she resides today in Wildomar. (Courtesy Nancy Jane Brown.)

The Wilks family residence on Palomar Road has a dirt road and row of palm trees in 1917. Tom Wilks, the alfalfa king, was a neighbor to the Brown family, as they lived only a half mile away. His children all attended Wildomar School along with the other families in the area. Like all of the pioneering families he participated in the active life of the community. (Courtesy Joe Tunstall.)

Theresa Wilks is holding baby Francis and watching Mary while standing in front of the Wilks barn in 1919. In the background, various wagon wheels are leaning against a workbench. The distinctive machine with teeth is a sickle mower. The wheels have a series of gear teeth to improve the action of the mowing. (Courtesy Joe Tunstall.)

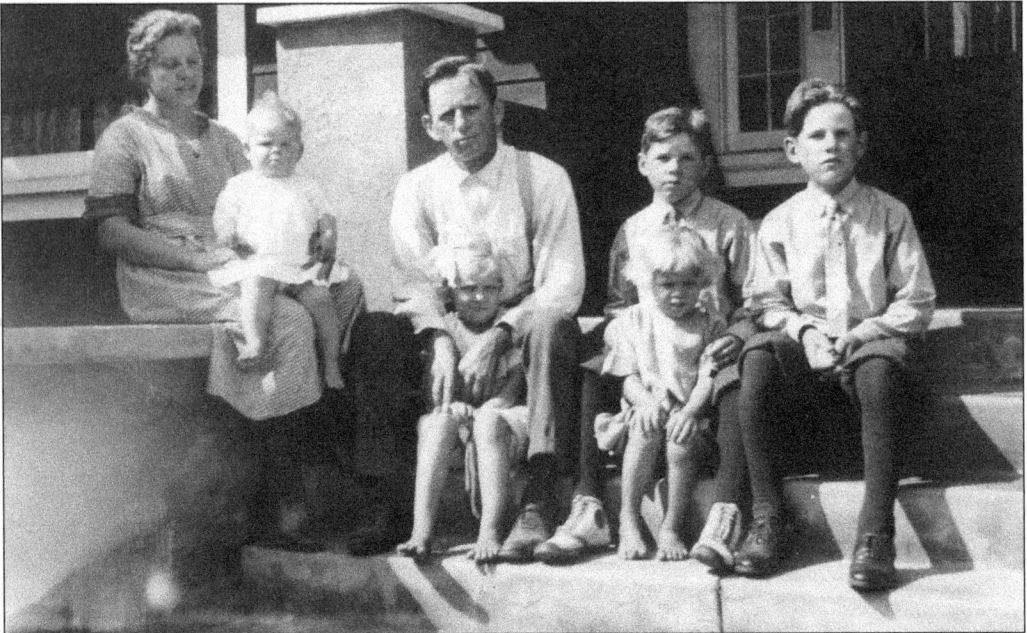

The Wilks family is sitting together in the summer of 1922 on the front porch of their Palomar Street house. As viewed from left to right, Horace, Evy, Art, Mary, and Francis are sitting with their parents, Theresa and Tom Wilks. There was one more child to be born, Tommy Wilks. This was not an unusual number of children for faming families of that era. (Courtesy Mary Wilks Gatch.)

Old farm equipment was always lying around the yard. The photograph shows a gathering of children and parents, including some Wilks family members, possibly on a Sunday afternoon. The clothes varied considerably, with some boys wearing farm clothes and others wearing white shirts and ties. To the left is the same mowing equipment in the 1919 photograph, so this photograph is likely from that era. (Courtesy Mary Wilks Gatch.)

Evelyn Wilks (Evy) is standing at the corner of the family house around 1935. Clothes for the family were not purchased. They were either hand-me-downs or sewn by their mother, Theresa Wilks. Evy eventually became adept at making her own clothes. (Courtesy Mary Wilks Gatch.)

Tommy Wilks was the youngest of the six children. He is pictured here shaking hands with Buster, the family dog. As the youngest child, his older brother's farm chores ultimately fell to him. Milking the cow was one of the chores that he had fun with, squirting the milk into the mouth of the waiting cat. (Courtesy Mary Wilks Gatch.)

The two-story Wilks house on Palomar Street around 1939 had four bedrooms and a sleeping porch upstairs. The downstairs consisted of three large front rooms—the dining room, a large living room with a wood stove, and a large kitchen with a kitchenette and pantry—along with an entrance hall, and a large screened porch for doing the laundry. With six children and occasional visitors, all of the space was utilized. (Courtesy Mary Wilks Gatch.)

With many of the children grown and a problem with termites and bees, the Wilks family decided to replace the old house with a modern home on top of the foundation of the old. Mary Wilks and two friends, Dolores and Agnes, pose in front of the new house in the mid to late 1940s. The same trees that were present in 1919 still line the driveway. (Courtesy Mary Wilks Gatch.)

Tom Wilks Sr. takes a few minutes to relax. The Wilks barn is visible in the background in this 1940 photograph. An inscription on the back of the picture says, "This is good." (Courtesy Mary Wilks Gatch.)

On the far left, Theresa Wilks is looking at the camera. The children are working the strawberry patch at the Wilks ranch in Wildomar in 1939. Gordon Gatch (back to camera) is looking to the hill at the south where Tommy Wilks eventually built his house. (Courtesy Mary Wilks Gatch.)

A spring fed the natural pool that was used as a stop for the Butterfield Stage and the Pony Express. Located on the old Wilks property, close to Palomar Street, the pool vanished after a well was drilled nearby. The pool has since been refilled. It is surrounded by 120-year-old pecan trees. (Courtesy Robert Cashman.)

The rural nature of the area is evident in this view of the B. F. Taylor house around 1930. A grape orchard is visible to the right of the house. (Courtesy John C. Taylor.)

46

Ben Taylor is at the right rear in front of three of his children in this two-family picture in 1915. Ben was a graduate of Wittenburg College in Springboro, Ohio, and served on the Wildomar School Board in the 1940s. Along with three others, in 1906 he came to Wildomar to farm 3,000 acres for William Collier. In addition to being a grain farmer, he was a turkey rancher for 50 years. (Courtesy John C. Taylor.)

As was the family tradition in 1917, a Christmas tree was set outside and decorated. B. F. Taylor had been doing carpentry on the house, which he hoped to finish before the rains came as he stepped over for this picture. In the photograph, Flossie is seated on the left, Jim and Frank are looking at each other, and Ellen (on the right) is interested in the three dolls she received for Christmas. (Courtesy John C. Taylor.)

The B. F. Taylor family stands on the side of the family house in 1924. The windows to the living room are on the left, and the windows to the dining room are on the right. Pictured here from left to right are (in front) Jim Taylor, Ellen Taylor, Frank Taylor; (back row) B. F. Taylor, Florence Taylor, and Fanny Taylor. (Courtesy John C. Taylor.)

Florence Taylor (Flossie) is about 18 years old, standing in front of the porch of the B. F. Taylor home in 1924 at the time of her high school graduation. Shadowed behind her in the window is (possibly) Ellen Taylor. (Courtesy John C. Taylor.)

This bird's-eye-view photograph was taken by Cal Taylor in 1953 of his father, Frank Taylor, and uncle Joe Shimmon repairing at the base of the windmill. Windmills were a part of the rural landscape since farmers and families found that water from the water company was more expensive than getting water from your own well. The windmill was about 30 feet tall, a standard steel tower with a small platform at the top. Water was pumped into a 500-gallon tank at an elevation of 20 or 25 feet. The water flowed to the kitchen faucets and some other faucets from an unpressurized tank. (Courtesy John C. Taylor.)

The Wildomar station replaced car "B" in 1886, which was set off on the northern side of the railroad tracks just northwest of Santa Rosa Street (now Clinton Keith Read). Car "B" had been used as the first depot in January 1884. Wildomar was originally on Santa Fe's transcontinental route to San Diego. Later, after the tracks were washed out, the line ended in Temecula. (Courtesy Robert Ambler.)

After the railroad line closed in 1935, cattle could still be delivered by truck. This ramp and loading dock was used to herd the cattle into the truck beds. It is located on McVicar Street near Grand Avenue. The picture shows the condition of the ramp in 2001. (Courtesy Jon Neal.)

Three

CHURCH, SCHOOL, AND BUSINESS

Social life in Wildomar centered around the churches, the Wildomar School, and, for a short time, the Wildomar Hotel. The Wildomar School opened in September 1886 with Alma Patterson as the teacher. The school was the site of community dances, plays, potluck suppers, and church meetings. One teacher who stood out as an educator was Iva Keegan who taught for 20 years in Wildomar. A famous item at the Wildomar School was the cast-iron bell in the tower. When the schoolhouse was torn down in 1951, the bell was removed and placed in a shrine in front of the school. In 2006, the shrine and bell were restored.

Wildomar was settled by Quakers, Presbyterians, and Episcopalians, each of whom had meeting places/churches in Wildomar. In the 1920s, other churches, including Lakeview Chapel, were started. Today Wildomar is home to 14 churches.

In the early 1900s, olives were important, and there was an olive cannery located in Lakeland Village. Some olive oil was also produced. Important industries over the years were feed stores, tack, watermelons, strawberries, walnuts, almonds, concord grapes, cattle, sheep, turkey and rabbit meat, and dairy. These industries are reflected in the names of Wildomar's streets, though the industries have long been gone.

Other industries from this era were gas stations and family eating establishments. A few of the important community gathering places over the years were the country stores—the Matthews Store, the Turner Wildomar Store, Nick's, and the Roundup Market.

The South Elsinore Department Corporation (SEDCO) promoted a townsite that opened on March 18, 1920. It was subdivided for small home farms dedicated to growing and selling deciduous fruit, citrus, walnut, almonds, and vegetables. Other businesses included apricots, eggs, and Whitney bottled water. This area was to become part of Wildomar.

Events in the 1940s through the 1960s included the World War II effort, repetitive flooding in the downtown area, the new post office, and the loss of the old Wildomar School. Wildomar continued to grow, adding the Elks building in 1983, Jean Hayman School in 1984, and the Wildomar Chamber of Commerce in 1990.

Wildomar School is seen in this picture from 1894. There are no trees or vegetation around the school. The teacher William Finley is standing behind his pupils. The first- and second-grade children are in the front and include Lex Muncy and George Embree, the first and second boys born in Wildomar. Other identified children include Helen Muncy, Lawrence, Clara Simmons, Pearl Wilson, Laura Henderson, Alida Pearson, Otta Finley, Arthur Hixon, and Archie Willets. (Courtesy David Turner.)

In 1927, Wildomar School was a one-room schoolhouse. Younger brothers and sisters were taught along with their elder siblings. This picture shows Francis and Mary Wilks, Wildfred Brown, twins Kathleen and David A. Brown, Joe and Carl Orvis, and Melvin and Velda Torbett as being in the same classroom. The teacher was Margaret Spear. The grades taught were first to eighth. (Courtesy David A. Brown.)

Wildomar School opened in September 1886 as a K-8 school with Alma Patterson as the teacher. The school was full to overflowing several years later. To accommodate the students, the school building was turned 90 degrees and a new, larger room added. A stage was added to the new room sometime before 1924, and a kitchen was added to the original room in the 1930s. The picture shows the two-room schoolhouse in 1945. (Courtesy Jean Hayman.)

In 1931, Wildomar School had two teachers; Iva Keegan taught the upper grades (left in photograph) and Mrs. McEntire taught the lower grades. The picture shows, in no particular order, Mary Wilks, Francis Wilks, Evelyn Wilks, Virginia Torbett, Nelda Torbett, Nina Jones, Earl Jones, Lucille, Ernst Orvis, June Miller, Jack Miller, Dick Miller, David Brown, Kathleen Brown, "Jerry" Brown, Kathleen Anspaugh, Margaret Anspaugh, Johnnie Clark, Jack Tarr, and Martin Reinbotsom. (Courtesy Jean Hayman.)

In the morning, schoolchildren lined up at the back entrance porch at the start of the school day, said the "Pledge of Allegiance," and marched into school. The main classroom had a bell tower and the back room was set up as a kitchen and dining room. With the arrival of the second teacher in 1945, it was converted into a classroom. The 55-gallon drum right outside the back window fueled the heater inside. (Courtesy David Turner.)

The 1948 Wildomar School sixth-grade class picture shows four students in the front row that walked from the fields with bare feet. In the seventh-grade class picture in 1949, all students wore shoes, and all the farm outfits had been replaced with better clothes. What a difference a year makes in the life of a teenager! (Courtesy Dorothy Davis.)

Nearly 500 residents and former residents of Wildomar gathered on Sunday, June 6, 1948, to honor Iva Keegan, who retired after 30 years of teaching, 20 years at Wildomar School. The school initially had one room but was a two-room schoolhouse at the time of her retirement. Iva is pictured in a black dress, second from right, wearing an orchid in her lapel. (Courtesy David Turner.)

Iva Keegan's retirement event was held at Wildomar School. Mrs. John Rodriquez, president of the mothers club, presided over beautifully arranged tea tables in the afternoon. Betty Turner, clerk of the board of the Wildomar School trustees, presided.

This is a star drill at the Wildomar School Christmas holiday program in the 1940s. Rachel Rodriquez, the girl in the foreground on the right in the darker clothing, is the only child identified on the back of the photograph. The green leafy branches on the ground are to be used in the program as oleanders. Color in the program was provided by the bright red berries and green lacy branches of the pepper trees. (Courtesy David A. Brown.)

Wildomar School is blanketed in snow on January 29, 1957. The school had a heater at the back of the classroom for cold weather. Older students had the privilege of sitting at the back of the class near the heater. The original school was torn down, and the lumber is supposed to be stored somewhere in Wildomar, but no one is really sure where. (Courtesy Stan Smith.)

The Wildomar School District was one of the 52 original school districts in Riverside County. In this October 1959 photograph, bus driver Gordon Hunt is showing the new school bus. The school district later was made a union district with the Lake Elsinore School District and lost the Wildomar designation. (Courtesy David Turner.)

A ladder is permanently nailed to the roof of the old Wildomar School. After many years of ringing, the bell developed a flat spot on the journal. The boys who got to ring the bell for good behavior were told not to ring it too vigorously, as the bell could seize up at the top and have to be released manually. The bell seized often enough that a ladder was thought to be necessary to provide an access for the boys to climb up and free the bell. (Courtesy Jean Hayman.)

WILDOMAR SCHOOL BELL
LAND DONATED BY
WILLIAM COLLIER &
DONALD GRAHAM
SCHOOL ERECTED SEPT. 1886
BELL LAST RANG JUNE 1958
PLAQUE PRESENTED BY
WILDOMAR HOME DEPT.
JUNE 1959

The bell that rang to open school each day was reportedly brought by train to Wildomar in 1886. The bell is 26 inches in diameter, 640 pounds, and was installed in the school tower. After the school was demolished, local residents built a shrine for it in front of the school. The present-day school and the bell monument are still at the original location of the first school, 21575 Palomar Street. (Courtesy Jon Neal.)

Ed Freeman is holding onto a nearly invisible screen as he works on the masonry for the simulated school tower in 1959. Rocks from a local quarry in Menifee and local rock from Wildomar were used for the base, and this plaque was embedded in the stone. The bell is located on the site of the original Wildomar School at Palomar Avenue and Central Street. (Courtesy David Turner.)

Ken Freeman is putting the finishing touches on the original shrine for the bell in 1959. Later a chain-link fence was added around the bell to protect it from birds (a major concern for a cast-iron bell due to the nitrates from their droppings) or from unscheduled bell tolling. When the bell was examined 50 years later, it was still in acceptable shape. (Courtesy David Turner.)

After 47 years of exposure, the wheel was no longer functioning and the cast-iron bell and frame were rusting. Wildomar Historical Society coordinators Bob Cashman and Vicki Long, along with Butterfield Trails coordinator Gary Andre, solicited and received donations of labor and money from the county and from residents and businesses that eagerly contributed. Kevin Wayne Zaradnik and Jimmy Lehto of KZ Masonry are shown in 2006 installing new stone over the original stone of the shrine.

The newly constructed monument in 2006 is waiting for the cast-iron bell and frame to come back from the powder coater. Once completed, the wheel was restored to enable the bell to be rung by pulling on a rope, as was done in the old schoolhouse. On incorporation day, July 1, 2008, the bell was officially rung, and the chimes of freedom announced the birth of a new city. (Courtesy Robert Cashman.)

Two time capsules were installed in the bell tower during its restoration in 2006. The capsules were painted by students attending Wildomar School. Todd Lee built the time capsules and the W at the top of the tower. Vacuum sealed bags are installed inside a bolted and sealed metal container to be opened in 50 years. (Courtesy Robert Cashman.)

The bell monument was completed, and a ceremony was held Christmas 2006. Bob Shaffer, Aurelio Gonzalez, Bob Cashman, Troy Smith, JoAnn Dykstra, Gary Andre, Todd Lee, Jim Lehto, Vicki and Larry Long, Steve Lusky, Carlos Stahl, Supervisor Bob Buster, Kevin Zaradnik, and various businesses donated over $25,000 in time and materials to construct an exceptionally sturdy monument. This monument could easily last another 100 years. (Courtesy Robert Cashman.)

The Margaret Collier Graham story, "The Complicity of Enoch Enbody," in *Sage Bloom and Water Rights: Stories of Early Southern California* by Many Moons Press contained this dialogue: " 'Is there a stopping place in this Burg?' He called out gaily. 'Thee'll find hotel up the street on thy right,' said Enoch. The stranger looked at him curiously, 'By gum, you're a Quaker.' " Quite possibly, this story used Wildomar as its setting. A large number of Quakers settled here, including William Edgerton, shown above. (Courtesy David Turner.)

Pastor Charles Willard of the Sedco Community Church stands by his 1932 Ford V-8 around 1934. The church at the time consisted of a Sunday school with occasional preaching by visiting ministers. There was no formal church building. (Courtesy Lakeview Chapel.)

Charles Wilson is pictured with his family around 1935. He was the pastor of the Sedco Community Church, which at the time was in a two-story house at the corner of Bundy Canyon Road and Mission Trail. (Courtesy Lakeview Chapel.)

The Sunday school class of Sedco Community Church is pictured in front of the building used for Sunday school in 1935. (Courtesy Lakeview Chapel.)

Sunday school teachers and students pose for this photograph in 1935. Superintendent Mrs. Frank Anderson, teachers Mr. and Mrs. Matson, Mrs. Nichols, Mrs. Bill Evans, and Chase Hall, among others, ran the school. Mrs. Matson was the pianist. (Courtesy Lakeview Chapel.)

Eunice England, wife of Pastor England, is in front of her house in 1936. Hidden by the trees is a car with a running board. (Courtesy Lakeview Chapel.)

In 1940, the missionary Rev. Charles Slater conducted a revival for the Sedco Community Church. A store building and the lot on which it stood was purchased for $300 and converted into a sanctuary. Lake View Chapel is shown under construction in 1941 at 32700 Mission Trail Road. The bell in the tower is the selfsame bell that had been used in the original Presbyterian church in Wildomar. (Courtesy Lakeview Chapel.)

The hallmark of Lakeview Chapel was its emphasis on evangelism. Guest missionaries conducted quarterly and later semiannual services, and an offering was taken for missions. Missionary Bob Hammond and his family pose for the camera at one of the all-day services in 1941. The Hammonds had a radio broadcast called *Voice of China and Asia.* (Courtesy Lakeview Chapel.)

Photographers used to travel from house to house with a pony for pictures. Jean Scherner (later Jean Hayman) poses on the pony in 1928. Though the Scherners lived in Elsinore, the reputation of Iva Keegen at Wildomar School was such that they sent their children, Jean, Robert, Dorothy, and Hazel, to get their education in Wildomar. The Scherner children attended Wildomar School for five years. (Courtesy Dorothy Davis.)

Henry Scherner was the owner and proprietor of the Elsinore Public Market on Main Street in Elsinore, as the city was called in those days. Main Street around 1928 was still dirt but with all those cars it must have been quite a busy commercial street. The market had a meat counter and a variety of canned goods. (Courtesy Dorothy Davis.)

Jean Margaret Scherner married Clarence Hayman, the chief of police in Elsinore, on February 12, 1953. Jean and Clarence Hayman are preparing to go out for a formal event on April 17, 1954. Many formal events in Elsinore and Wildomar were connected either to the churches or to the Masonic orders. Jean Hayman was a royal matron, order of the Eastern Star, Elsinore Chapter 243. (Courtesy Dorothy Davis.)

Patty Di Giacomo, Horace Whisment, Paul Chamberlain, Jimmy Abbott, and Mary Soseby serenade their teacher, Jean Hayman, on the opening day of school in September 1959. Jean Hayman graduated from the University of Southern California with a degree in music. (Courtesy Dorothy Davis.)

Students are seated during the 1945–1946 school term at Elsinore Union Grammar School. Rows of individual desks and a chalkboard define the classroom setting for the new teacher. (Courtesy Dorothy Davis.)

Dr. Ron Flora, Dave Struthers, and trustees Sonja Wilson and Chuck Sisco applaud Jean Hayman at the ground-breaking ceremony for the Jean Hayman School on 21440 Lemon Street in Wildomar on March 3, 1984. Jean Hayman was the only teacher who began her teaching career and taught her entire 39-year career in the local school district. The school was closed temporarily in 2006. (Courtesy Jean Hayman.)

Since Riverside County did not officially recognize the flooding as an emergency, it was considered the responsibility of the homeowner to protect his own property. Billy Stevenson, Gerry Stevenson, and Bryan Stevenson lay sandbags around their house in 1979. More than 1,000 sandbags were used. (Courtesy Gerry Stevenson.)

LeRoy and Bob Stevenson drag tumbleweeds to the front of the house to shore up the berm on Gruwell Street during the flooding of 1979. The previous flooding in 1978 had brought Darby and Central Street to the point where 14 people had to be evacuated from their homes and housed at Wildomar School. (Courtesy Gerry Stevenson.)

This is the view down Gruwell Street toward Grand Avenue in early 1980. The county generated berm is 7 to 8 feet high, and water was cascading down the street like a river. It was the continual flooding of the downtown area that resulted in the formation of the Wildomar Interest League (WIL) in 1979. (Courtesy Gerry Stevenson.)

A wave of water is traveling down Gruwell Street during the flooding in 1980. The berm protecting the houses is over 7 feet high. Those living along Gruwell Street at Pecan, Dunn, and Darby Streets saw their road erode and wash away. The flooding led to the appointment of David A. Brown as the Zone 7 flood control commissioner. (Courtesy Gerry Stevenson.)

In 1980, back-to-back 100-year rainfall resulted in flooding. Lake Elsinore overflowed its banks for the first time since 1916, flooding the adjacent airport on the floodplain and the buildings in Sedco along Mission Trail Road. Pictured is the damage to Skylark Airport. To prevent further damage to Sedco, a 5-foot-high dike was constructed along Mission Trail Road adjacent to the lake. (Courtesy Anne Sullivan School.)

Before the flood control channel was built, water found its way down dry rivers. Shown above is the dry river in 1980 near the present-day Anne Sullivan School. The ability to carry water during heaving rainfall was limited. Of course, as these children from the school illustrate, it was not all bad. You could always play in the dry riverbed. (Courtesy Anne Sullivan School.)

LeRoy and Gerry Stevenson are standing at the corner of Darby and Gruwell Streets during the flooding in March 1983. Gerry is taking notes and preparing for another battle with the county for effective flood control in Wildomar. The solution offered by the Wildomar Interest League was to use the old railroad bed in Wildomar as the site for a flood control channel. (Courtesy Gerry Stevenson.)

When flooding was severe in the area between Palomar and Grand Streets, including near the elementary school and the post office, cars sometimes had to be pulled out of the water when their engines flooded out. It could be a real adventure to get mail from the post office. This photograph was taken on March 4, 1983, on Gruwell Street. (Courtesy Gerry Stevenson.)

The original Wildomar Cemetery was located in a rocky plot of land on lot 18, block S. The townspeople of Wildomar donated funds to move all of the coffins except the one holding Joseph Nichols. It stood by itself, surrounded by an ornate iron fence with a marble head and footstone, for 90 years. The other graves were moved in 1898 to the cemetery on Palomar Street. (Courtesy David A. Brown.)

The fence around his grave was moved intact by volunteers including Joe Jeffries and David Brown. Joseph Nichols was a stationmaster for the Santa Fe Railroad. After being jilted by the girl he loved, he took his own life by shooting himself with a handgun. Only one arm was found in the casket, leading credence to the story that he was one-armed. (Courtesy Nancy Jane Brown.)

David A Brown is using a skip loader to move the headstone. One story as to why Joseph's grave was not moved in 1898 is that as a suicide he could not be buried on hallowed ground. Another story is that the citizens were waiting for the woman dressed in black who attended his funeral to come forward and pay for the move to the new cemetery. (Courtesy Nancy Jane Brown.)

The final resting place of Joseph Nichols is in the Wildomar Cemetery at 21400 Palomar Street. A small ceremony was held at the site of the new grave an April 4, 1979. The 4-H Kountry Kids solemnly saluted the flag, flowers were bought to the site by interested townspeople, and Marna O'Brien led a prayer for the peace of Joseph Nichols. (Courtesy Rich and Sue Skinner.)

Washing of the grave markers is an annual event in Wildomar. The girl scouts and their leaders are helping to clean the dirt that has accumulated over the year off the gravestones. The gravestone that is upright at the left is the second oldest in the cemetery; Mary Wilks died in 1886.

Located at the corner of the north corner of Central Avenue and Palomar Street, this structure was built in 1910. It was used as a gas station/motel in Wildomar from 1933 until about 1979. A pillar on the corner of the building has a conical light on top. It served as the home for the Wildomar Food Sharing Center in the early 1980s. (Courtesy Riverside Park and Open Space District.)

In April 1958, this view of the structure at the north corner of Central and Palomar Streets, "Gagnon Corner" as it was called at that time, highlights the iris plants behind the Turners' Wildomar Store. Many varieties of iris are drought tolerant in the shade. The building, originally built in 1910, had a restaurant, gas station, and a small mechanics garage. This made Wildomar a two gas station town! (Courtesy David Turner.)

The Turner store on Palomar Street near Central Street is busy in 1942. The store was not large but included a small meat area, a small milk shake shop with three seats, and a good assortment of everything else including medicines, canned and fresh foods, candy, and cigarettes. The sign above the door says, "groceries, meats, cold drinks, ammunition, and drugs." The other sign reads "Post Office, Wildomar." (Courtesy David Turner.)

In the 1940s, gas was 15¢ a gallon. The two gas pumps both had 10 gallon glass containers on top. You hand pumped the gas into them (marked quantity lines) and then gravity flow hosed it into your gas tank. In this picture, there is no garage behind the gas station. The station was located next to Turner's Store. (Courtesy David Turner.)

The Turners decided to rent out the filling station and garage that was next to their store to mechanics. In this picture from the late 1950s, the gas pumps are electric and no longer depend on gravity feed. There were just two types of gas, ethyl and regular. (Courtesy David Turner.)

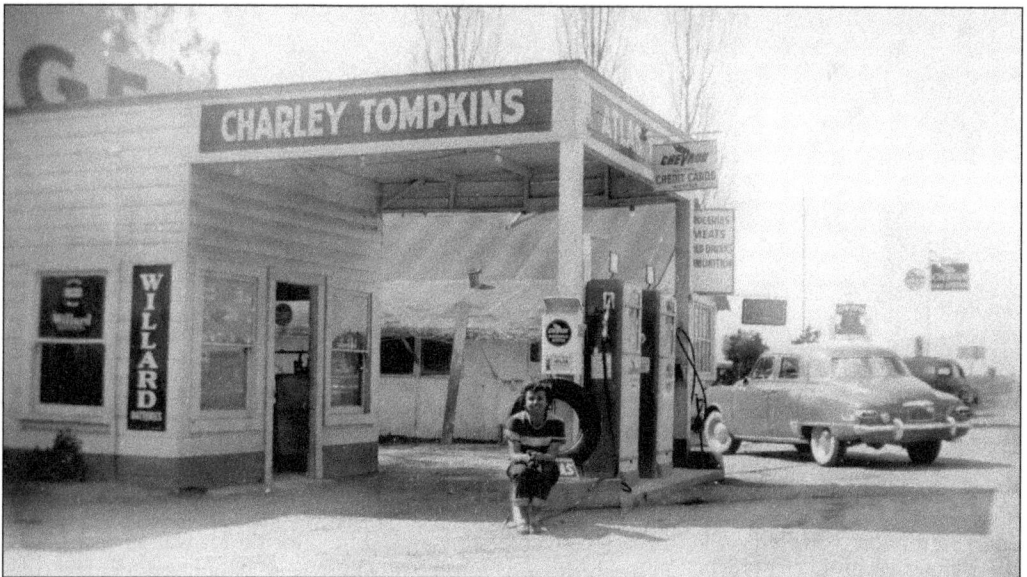

In 1949, Charles Tompkins ran this garage and filling station near the corner of Central and Palomar Streets, immediately adjacent to Turner's Wildomar Store and Real Estate. The girl sitting by the gas pumps is Judy Tompkins Kathriner. (Courtesy Rose Tompkins.)

A review of the records kept by William Collier and subsequently by David Brown found 14 periods of snow in Wildomar, from light dusting to 9 inches. This calculates out to a snowfall about every eight years. In 1957, the snow was almost a foot deep. On the left side of the photograph, by the Wildomar store and filling station, are the poles used to carry power to downtown Wildomar. (Courtesy Stan Smith.)

Nick's was located at the curve where Palomar Street becomes Mission Trail and was a little country market, somewhat like today's convenience stores. The parking lot was surfaced with decomposed granite (DG) and had hitching posts out front. There were benches under the trees where you could sit outside and talk. There was no air-conditioning inside the store, so it was quite hot during the summer. Outside, multiple newspaper racks, a community note board, and a pay phone are visible. (Courtesy Wildomar Chamber of Commerce.)

Nick's was completely rebuilt and opened as Wildomar Round Up Liquor and Grocery, Feed, and Pet Supply under the ownership of the Bailiff family. The store is shown right after opening day in 1985. Curly Bailiff was the vice president and general manager. Sally Bailiff ran the deli. Two horses are hitched outside to the right of the store. The horseshoe pit is not visible in the photograph. (Courtesy Wildomar Chamber of Commerce.)

In the late 1940s, advertising signs for soft drinks are posted on the side of Highway 71 in Wildomar on the way to Lake Elsinore. Pictured are signs for Royal Crown Cola, Coca-Cola, and 7Up. (Courtesy David Turner.)

The fire station opened in 1981 at 32637 Gruwell Street on a half acre of land donated by Dave Turner. Engine 61 was put into service in November 1980 even before the one-engine station was built. The station was manned by the Wildomar Volunteer Fire Company. (Courtesy Jon Neal.)

The Turners' home, the Wildomar Store, and the Wildomar Post Office were side by side as shown above. Whether it was helping at the Wildomar School that was across the street, handing out the mail, reconditioning the cemetery, or helping families with problems, they always had time to work to make this a better place for the whole community. (Courtesy David Turner.)

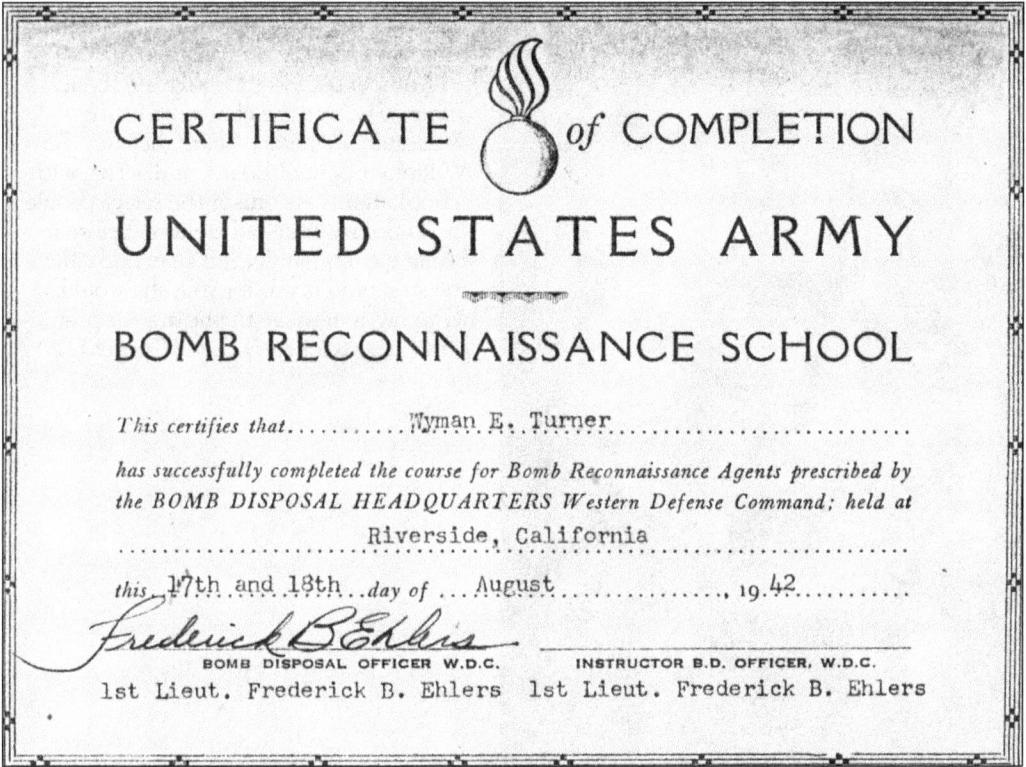

CERTIFICATE of COMPLETION

UNITED STATES ARMY

BOMB RECONNAISSANCE SCHOOL

This certifies that.......... Wyman E. Turner ....

has successfully completed the course for Bomb Reconnaissance Agents prescribed by
the BOMB DISPOSAL HEADQUARTERS Western Defense Command; held at
Riverside, California

this 17th and 18th day of ... August ...., 19 42 ....

Frederick B Ehlers

BOMB DISPOSAL OFFICER W.D.C.   INSTRUCTOR B.D. OFFICER, W.D.C.
1st Lieut. Frederick B. Ehlers   1st Lieut. Frederick B. Ehlers

Betty and Wyman Turner were involved in many volunteer organizations during the emergency war years of 1941–1945. In 1942, Wyman was designated as the "air raid warden" for Wildomar. He received special training on bomb disposal in case bombs fell in Wildomar. That never happened, but he was able to put his training to use checking out and defusing one of the Japanese balloon bombs that landed on the Santa Rosa Plateau. (Courtesy David Turner.)

Betty and Wyman Turner manned the Ground Observer Corps (GOC) post in Wildomar at their store continuously, 24 hours a day for the more than four years that the GOC was in operation during World War II. Their report, which included spotting and identifying planes, went to the filter center in Santa Ana. For their work, they were each awarded a Meritorious Service Award from the U.S. Air Force Ground Observer Corps. (Courtesy David Turner.)

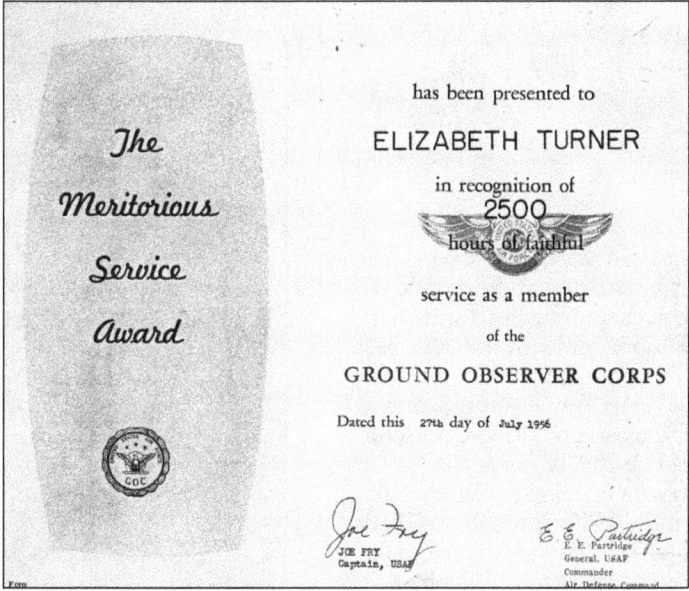

The Meritorious Service Award

has been presented to

ELIZABETH TURNER

in recognition of
2500
hours of faithful

service as a member

of the

GROUND OBSERVER CORPS

Dated this 27th day of July 1956

Joe Fry
JOE FRY
Captain, USAF

E. E. Partridge
E. E. Partridge
General, USAF
Commander
Air Defense Command

Betty Turner not only ran the Wildomar Store and was the postmistress of the post office, but also was active in civic affairs. She was the chairman of the Wildomar Cemetery Board, head of the Wildomar School Board, and active with school affairs. As one of the select people in Wildomar who had a phone before it became commonplace, if someone called the store and it was for you, she would write out a message to put in your post office box. (Courtesy David Turner.)

In 1947, Wyman and Betty Turner had the unusual distinction of both being the head of their Masonic order in the same year. This photograph was taken for Wyman Turner's installation as the master of Elsinore Masonic Lodge 289. Wyman, the unofficial mayor of Wildomar in the 1940s through the 1960s, and his wife were a force to be reckoned with in Wildomar.

Bruce De Marce, a field service officer for the U.S. Post Office Department in this area, is waiting to give his talk, dedicate the new location for the Wildomar Post Office, and hand cancel the first letter. The ribbon was cut and the flag raised over the new post office building located at the corner of the old Highway 395 and Central Avenue on March 26, 1961, at 2:00 p.m. (Courtesy David Turner.)

The post office in 1961 was right next to Turner Store. It was built over the foundation of the old garage after it burned to the ground. The post office before that time was in the Wildomar Store. Between the two of them, the Turners ran the post office for 38 years. Wyman Turner was postmaster from 1942 to 1965, and Betty Turner was postmistress from 1965 to 1980. (Courtesy David Turner.)

Betty Turner and son Dave Turner are at her home standing on bricks from the old school building in about 1982. After his father passed away, Dave Turner took over the real estate business and ran Turner Realty from 1979 to 1982. (Courtesy David Turner.)

The Turner Realty building at 21545 Palomar was the former Wildomar Store on Palomar Street with an additional wing added to the building. The signature red roses had not yet been planted in front of the office. This was Dave Turner's main real estate office, featuring "the best in country property since 1945." Turner Realty ultimately had five offices; two in Wildomar, one in Elsinore, one in Murrieta, and one in Temecula. (Courtesy David Turner.)

Wyman Turner and Carl Mansfield are working on the fireworks launch site for the first fireworks over Lake Elsinore on July 4, 1948. Wyman was the initiator and leader behind the event for the first years. Behind the two men is the nearly dry lake bed of Lake Elsinore. (Courtesy David Turner.)

This is the east view of the new post office at 21549 Palomar Street, which was dedicated in 1961. A hallmark of the post office was the large number of post office boxes. Retrieving mail was almost a social event. In 1979, they actually ran out of post office boxes, and the new residents had to get their mail across the counter at "general delivery." More boxes were added to remedy the situation.(Courtesy David Turner.)

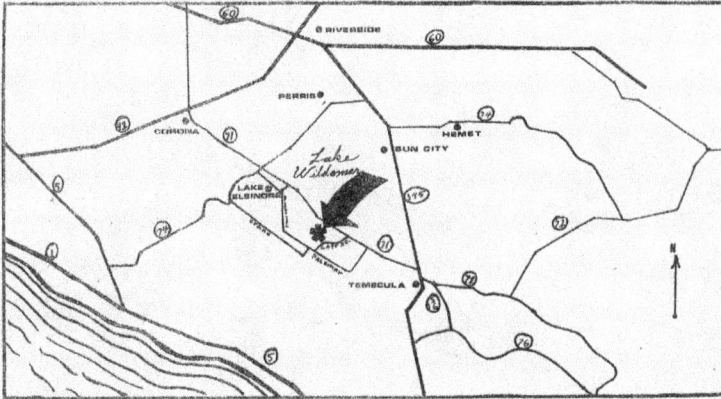

Lake Wildomar
Recreation Vehicle Park
and Campground

6 Miles South of Lake Elsinore
on Hwy. 71. Turn Right
on Catt Road.

P.O. Box 197
23120 Catt Rd.
Wildomar, Calif. 92395

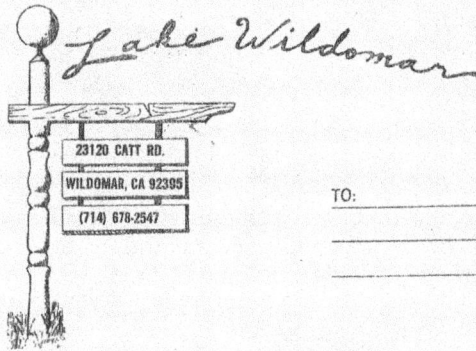

(714) 678-2547

23120 CATT RD.
WILDOMAR, CA 92395
(714) 678-2547

TO:

PLACE
POSTAGE
HERE

Lake Wildomar

FISHING LAKE
SWIMMING POOL
CAMPING

COUNTRY STORE
REC. ROOM
PICNICKING

Lake Wildomar was an RV Park and campground. Located at 23130 Catt Road, it had an Olympic-sized pool, a stocked fishing lake, a country store, a playground, and a dance floor that could hold 15 squares. Special rates were available for day camping and club groups. The normal rates were $50 per month for full hookup, $27.50 for each week, or $4.50 per day for four people.

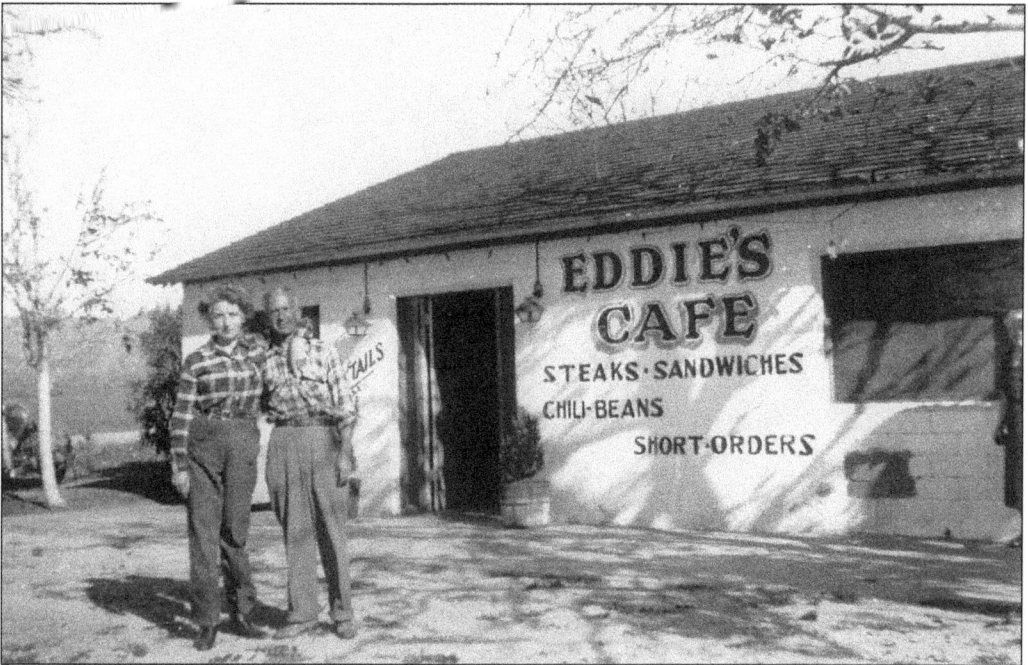

In 1938, Eddie's Cafe fronted on Palomar Street, also known as Highway 395. The cafe was later sold, remodeled, and a new facade was added. The new owners, Jim and Eve, called it Eve's Cafe. (Courtesy Susan Morgan.)

The building is remodeled and open for business as Eve's Cafe. Streets in those days were identified by carved letters on street posts. The post to the left of the photograph is marked Cyn Dr. and Mission Trail. Canyon Drive is a dirt street in 1938. Mission Trail is paved, as it was also State Highway 395. The building was opposite the present Mission Trail Library. (Courtesy Susan Morgan.)

Peacocks on the property functioned as guard birds. The peacocks were a local sight at Eve's Cafe long after it had closed. They took residence in the yard and successfully fended for themselves. They could often be seen on the roof of the closed cafe when driving down Palomar Street. (Courtesy Susan Morgan.)

JIM and EVE'S CAFE

Famous for Southern Fried Chicken and Fine Steaks

Open Daily Except Monday and Tuesday

Telephone 2312
On Highway 395

4½ Miles South of
Elsinore, California

Travelers that heard of the famous southern fried chicken made sure that they stopped on their way through the area. It was a favorite meeting place for locals who stopped by for conversation and food. This advertisement is from a 1957 Elsinore High School yearbook. (Courtesy Herman DeJong.)

Eve's Cafe had a long mahogany and glass bar that had been imported intact from an establishment in Nevada. Beside the bar was a large, wood dance floor. Square dances, casual dancing, and live music were common. Outside of Eve's Cafe was a patio area that was landscaped and set with lights for evening gatherings. (Courtesy of Susan Morgan.)

Eve stands in front of the log cabin she built, one of three known to be constructed in Wildomar. The mud and wood construction is visible on the wall behind her. (Courtesy of Susan Morgan.)

Originally built in 1922 by the son of Franklin Heald, one of the founders of Lake Elsinore, the ranch house was located at 35880 Frederick Street. The structure had a composition and sheet metal gable roof. The Heald ranch in Wildomar was comprised of 58.95 acres and located off of Frederick Street and Catt Road. It was photographed on September 16, 1981. (Courtesy Riverside Park and Open Space District.)

With the need to control runoff water, detention basins were made to handle the increased flow resulting from development. Jewell Flinn, a dryland farmer who also worked for the Riverside County Soil Conservation, is grading in 1948. The grading equipment is seen at a site located off of Grand Avenue. (Courtesy Gloria Smith.)

The Wildomar Chamber of Commerce was founded in 1990. Their logo was designed as a result of a contest run by the chamber. The three figures on the hill are representations of Wildomar's three founders—Donald Graham, William Collier, and Margaret Collier Graham. The letters in Wildomar replace their eyes to suggest that they see the future Wildomar as they look over the valley. Wildomar School with its tower and bell is on the right side, representing education. On the left side, the Butterfield Stage travels away from the Wildomar of today. The motto adopted by the chamber is "the doors of tradition open to the future."

Wildomar Wild West Fest

You'All Come Now, y'Hear?

Saturday & Sunday
July 13 & 14

Baxter Exit Off I-15
Follow Central to Palomar

- FUN FOR THE ENTIRE FAMILY! -

18 Acres of Food & Fun!

* Wild West Stunt Show
* Entertainment • Games • Prizes
* Children's Fair • Pony Rides • Petting Farm
* Tug - O - War
* Arts & Crafts
* Business Expo

The Music of
- Shorty Robins & The Wildomar Riders -

Kids!
Come See Dizzy Darla

** SAVE $1 **
Pre-sale tickets just $3 each!
Seniors $2 • Children under 5 FREE
For information call 678-7839

k-hi 105.7

Sponsored by the Wildomar Chamber of Commerce

Between 1:00 a.m. on Saturday and 7:00 p.m. on Sunday, a crowd of over 5,000 people from all around Southern California came through the gates of the 18-acre grounds for the first Wild West Fest sponsored by the Wildomar Chamber of Commerce in 1991. There were 61 arts, crafts, and commercial booths along with seven food vendors, live music, and many other amusements. The event was put together by Diane and Kurt Larson of Brit AM. The festivities were presided over by chamber president Gary Brown. The Wild West Fest returned in 1992, 1993, and 1995.

The fourth Wildomar Wild West Fest took place in 1995 in a field located between the I-15 freeway and Monte Vista. The event was sponsored by the Wildomar Chamber of Commerce.

Dirt byways, heat, and dust did not deter the crowds who enjoyed the Wild West Fest with its music, performances, and gunfighters (the temperature was over 105 degrees Fahrenheit). In their spare time, guests could visit the tractors, drink soft drinks or beer, listen to the music, and visit the booths operated by various vendors.

Work on Elks Lodge 2591 was started in 1983 with supervision of the area for proper permits. Dedicated in 1984, the building had been in continuous use since then for activities such as jazz, polka, community dinners, and other events. Elks Lodge 2591 donated more than $50,000 annually for charitable community projects. Unfortunately, the lodge burned to the ground in an early morning three-alarm fire on November 7, 2007. (Courtesy Paul Niehouse Sr.)

In 1983, Emal Smith, Elmer Bozanth, and Milo Gilbert help prepare the foundation for cement flooring for the new lodge at 33700 Mission Trail in Wildomar. All labor was donated, and Ernal Smith, who owned the Ready Mix Company, purchased the cement mix at owners cost. Two older buildings are seen in the background on the property where the VFW post would later be built. (Courtesy Paul Niehouse Sr.)

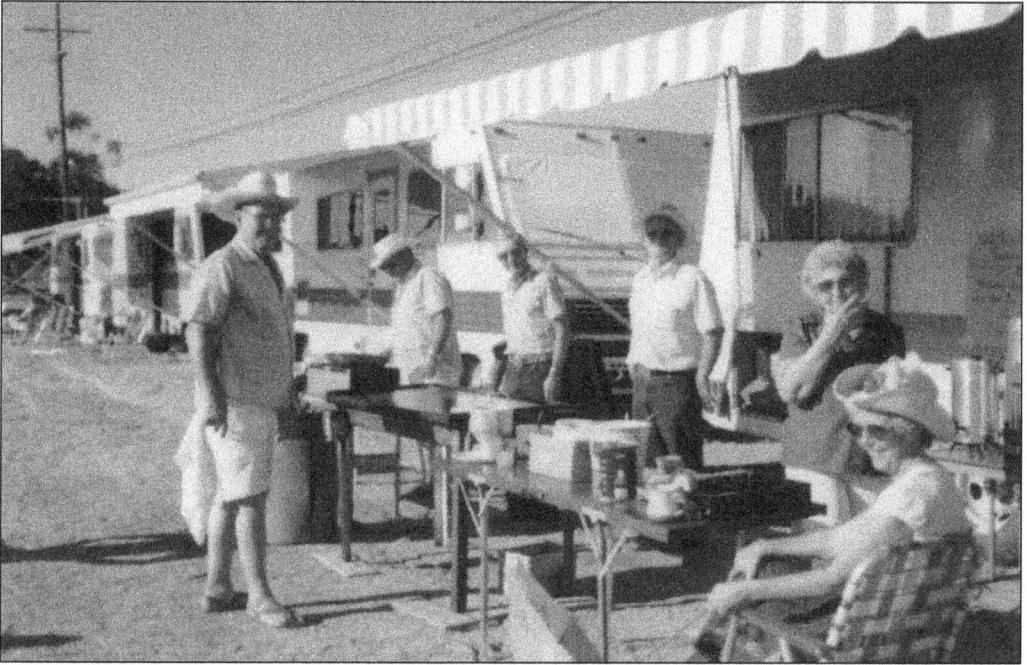

Elks members parked their mobile homes on the property so they could watch the property and building. Someone was always cooking meals for the day. After working, there was a social relaxation time every evening. Jim and Myrtle Payne, Fran Chambers, and Clint and Cordy Taylor are shown by their mobile homes. (Courtesy Paul Niehouse Sr.)

Country and Western music was played all day by Roy Hortchar and Band, who donated their time. Using the flatbed of a truck for a stage was a great idea, as it lifted the band above the ground noise. This same type of stage was used in 1995 for the Wild West Fest in Wildomar. (Courtesy Paul Niehouse Sr.)

The building crew was composed of all volunteers. John Hunter, Tom Richardson, Mareta Richardson, Del Karl, Harry Yanover, Vern Richardson, Bill Davis, and other Elks members tend to the framing of the 6,800 square foot facility. Elks Lodge 2591 was originally located at Four Corners in Elsinore and was called the Lake Elsinore Lodge when it was built in Wildomar. The name of the lodge changed to Lake Elsinore/Wildomar lodge in 2008. (Courtesy Paul Niehouse Sr.)

In the 1890s, Wildomar already had water pumped in to the main part of town. Pipes from the reservoir on the hillside above Grand Avenue supplied the water. After the system was no longer being used in the 20th century, it was a great place for boys to swim after school or to fish for bluegill. It was great fun in the summertime. (Courtesy David Turner.)

Four

RANCHES AND HOUSING TRACTS

Independent ranches and farms have been a part of Wildomar since the 1880s. Families would buy 5 to 20 acres and establish their own piece of paradise, usually concentrating on one of the agricultural industries. Farming is not an easy life, but it did allow a husband and wife to live the American dream, which included a home of their own and a family. Hundreds of these little ranches were scattered around the area, and some even remain today. In a number of instances, a family would live in rough surroundings, possibly a tent or a barn, while building their house. A few families cast their houses out of adobe bricks, made from straw, and the clay found on their property. Several of these houses remain to this day.

Since Donald Graham and William Collier subdivided Wildomar in 1884, there remained a larger number of half-acre or larger parcels that have been settled on, many with modular or mobile homes. This has retained some of the rural character of the area.

In addition to the businesses (such as feed and hay stores, honey processing, construction firms, dairy farms, and water bottling), a line of horse ranches, including Rafter T Ranch, Archer Ranch, Circle H Ranch, and Rancho Fortunado lay along Palomar and Grand Avenues at the southern end of Wildomar. Rancho Fortunado specialized in racehorses and had a track for jockeys to train with their horses. Wildomar was not yet a city, so the county had the zoning responsibility. With the county rezoning of Wildomar, these ranches gradually vanished, slowly being replaced with housing tracts. Elsewhere in Wildomar, there is still a thriving horse-related industry.

The completion of I-15 through the area in 1982 led to the first major housing tract, Windsong Valley, located off of the I-15 freeway and Baxter Road. Shopping markets opened on Clinton Keith Road to serve this larger population. This has created a mix of old and new in Wildomar.

In 1979, the property west of the I-15 freeway and south of Baxter Road was open fields that were about to be transformed into a housing tract. The Windsong housing tract, located off the Baxter Road exit ramp on the I-15 freeway, was the first major housing development to take place in Wildomar. This development was a direct consequence of expectations generated by the building of the I-15 freeway to replace Highway 71. (Courtesy Anne Sullivan School.)

This is a view looking east from Anne Sullivan School in 1988 toward the same piece of property that is shown in the previous picture. Hay bales have turned into two-story houses in the Windsong tract. A drainage problem is evident on the adjacent property. (Courtesy Anne Sullivan School.)

In 1987, the first house in the Windsong tract was yet to be built. The wide open feeling of Wildomar's past is still evident. Marlene Messaros and her dog are looking with interest at the property where their house will be built. Different phases of this housing development eventually gave way to over 2,000 homes. (Courtesy Marlene Messaros.)

48 ACRE HORSE RANCH SITE

LAMKIN RANCH

WILDOMAR, CALIFORNIA

Located in

WILDOMAR - MURRIETA VALLEY

Southern California

A well known, fast growing horse ranching area

It was this advertisement that brought the Sukhov's to Wildomar. Three of the six Sukhov children, Boris, Alex, and Vladimir, transformed this beat-up Thoroughbred facility into a premier horse ranch that featured Thoroughbred racing. They named their ranch Rancho Fortunado, a name for the area that was taken from an old map from the late 1880s. (Courtesy Alex Sukhov.)

Vladimir Sukhov is farming oat hay and alfalfa on his tractor at Rancho Fortunado in 1978. Hard work and diligence were needed to make this a great place to live. At the Grand Avenue side of the property, an old cattle ramp remained from the days when the land was used for cattle ranching. (Courtesy Alex Sukhov.)

The oat hay crop from Rancho Fortunado in 1978 extended from McVicar and Grand Streets to Palomar Street. The land could support two or three crops per year if the planting and harvesting were done at the right time. For about four years, the family ran a quarantine area for expensive ($500,000–$1 million) horses that needed to be isolated for a month before being flown to areas all over the world. (Courtesy Alex Sukhov.)

Nicolai Sukhov left Russia in 1917, married Roza, and ultimately immigrated to the United States, the land of opportunity. Their house was located on 18 acres at Rancho Fortunado, where they raised chickens, lambs, fruit, vegetables (especially tomatoes for homemade pasta), and an occasional cow or horse. Sheep are grazing on the alfalfa crop on the ranch in 1982. (Courtesy Alex Sukhov.)

In this aerial view of Rancho Fortunado in 1980, the five-eighths-mile oval racetrack is next to a 49 stall barn off of Palomar and McVicar Streets. The upper 18 acres of the ranch were purchased in 1974 with an additional 45 acres in 1978. The ranch was operational for 30 years. The David A. Brown ranch house is on 35 acres, and pictured on the left upper side of the photograph. (Courtesy Kathy Pierce.)

The DeJong family takes a short vacation in 1957 just before they started their dairy business in Wildomar. Starting a new business is quite an undertaking, so there were a few lean years at the start. (Courtesy Herman DeJong.)

John and Kate DeJong first opened the Wildomar Dairy in 1958 on the south side of Central Avenue near Dunn Street. They started with one cow and, within a few years, had a dairy with a thriving milk delivery route across the valley. In 1961, the dairy was moved to its present 32-acre location at 31910 Corydon Road. There was plenty of work to keep the whole family busy. (Courtesy Herman DeJong.)

The agriculture teacher is checking up on Pete DeJong's beef in the 1960s. Future Farmers of America still has a chapter at Elsinore High School (located in Wildomar). The dairy is an old-fashioned agriculture business. Herman still breeds and raises his own cows and does not use any hormones to increase milk production. (Courtesy Herman DeJong.)

Herman and Marilyn took over the dairy's operation in 1971 from Herman's father, John DeJong. Herman is seen in the delivery truck at the time. In 1974, the dairy sold an average of 200 gallons a day. DeJong's dairy is the only remaining "cash and carry" dairy in Riverside County. Since it is not part of the state's "milk pool," they are not allowed to produce more than 500 gallons a day. (Courtesy Herman DeJong.)

The Sedco Hills Clubhouse was the center of social activity for the Sedco area. One corner of the building is visible in the upper right of the photograph. The structure was located on Orchard east of the intersection with Muscatel Street. Based on the vintage of the cars, this photograph must have been taken about 1957. (Courtesy of John Cantacessi.)

Owner and builders Arthur and Lupe Mejia stand in the midst of the construction project. The property had a barn when it was purchased, so construction of a water tower and the house in 1955 was a top priority. The house is located at 31950 Central Avenue just before it becomes Baxter Road. (Courtesy Mary Ellen Robbins.)

Successful farming meant having a variety of animals and crops. On this 5-acre piece of paradise, water was pumped from a well to a large storage tank at the back of the house. Cattle were slaughtered, and the meat was sold to local meat markets. A double tanning bed was cast in concrete and set behind the house to tan hides. (Courtesy Mary Ellen Robbins.)

Commercial orange groves were not common in Wildomar, since the stream beds and the hills were in different climatic zones. Joe Cantacessi shows off a Valencia orange tree on his property in 1948. (Courtesy John Cantacessi)

In 1960, veteran turkey raiser Joe Cantacessi shows some handsome tom turkeys that survived a Thanksgiving custom because they had been selected for breeding purposes. The Cantacessi's raised between 4,000 and 5,000 turkeys a year on a 30-acre ranch on Canyon Drive. They did their own breeding and settled on a particular large bronze breed. Walnut trees on the property shaded the turkeys during the summer heat. (Courtesy John Cantacessi.)

Turkeys have been raised on a number of farms in Wildomar since the early 1900s. Joe Cantacessi is standing with his grandsons on the family farm in 1968. Pictured on the left is Cantacessi's grandson Anthony, and on the right is his grandson Joe, holding the ax at the chopping block. Poor turkey! (Courtesy John Cantacessi.)

This house at the Marna O'Brien Park at 20505 Palomar Street was originally the farmhouse for the 35-acre Bill and Mabel Wright Turkey Farm. The property was purchased by the Ortega Trails Recreation District (now disbanded). The Wright ranch house was converted into an office, and playgrounds were put outside. The house was later demolished as part of the construction of the park by the county.

The first of five houses is under construction. Gerry, Eddie, and Olive Pelletier rest against the building after a day of construction in 1944. The house was located at Corydon Street and Grand Avenue and was finished in 1945. In 1947, they started building their second house on Robert Road. Pete also built the Valley Inn on Grand Avenue and put the tower on the 1959 bell shrine. (Courtesy Gerry Moncur.)

The Pelletier family lived in a tent while building their first house in 1945 on Robert Road. This was not unusual as people simply did what was necessary and no code enforcement bothered them. Wildomar founders, Donald Graham and Margaret Collier Graham, also lived in a tent while the family was building their home in South Pasadena in the 1900s. (Courtesy Gerry Moncur.)

The Pelletier family takes time out during construction of the house in 1945. Pictured here are, from left to right, Eddie, Gerry (on Colonel), Olive, Millie, and Elroy (Pete). (Courtesy Gerry Moncur.)

Corydon Street and Grand Avenue are pictured as seen from the ranch house in 1945. (Courtesy Gerry Moncur.)

In this 1980 photograph, the entrance to Whitney Water at 21190 Sedco Boulevard, the corner of Sedco Boulevard and Lakeview Terrace, is announced by a sign that advertises the coin operated water dispenser to the right in the photograph. Two gallons of water were sold for 75¢. It was advertised as "fresh daily since 1959." (Courtesy Denise Sewell.)

The "deep well" was drilled in 1955 to a depth of 310 feet. With a capacity of 450 gallons a minute, enough water was produced for the bottling business. George Whitney had studied at Frank Wiggins trade school, so he decided to put his skills to use as the painter of the valley, specializing in signs (like this one) and in painting the interiors of buildings. (Courtesy Denise Sewell.)

The Whitney's delivery truck is on the left side of the picture. The water bottling unit is being moved. Whitney water comes from the deep well. No water from the lake is bottled. (Courtesy Denise Sewell.)

Aeration is essential to keep the lake cleaned. Initially advertised as a fishing paradise for members only, Whitney's Lake and Recreation was a perfect weekend getaway. The lake was stocked with largemouth and smallmouth bass and blue gill with an occasional stocking of rainbow trout. The water business triumphed over the recreation business, and the pond was closed to the public. Palm trees ring the outside of this man-made lake. Large metal aviaries beside the lake housed hundreds of parrots, rare birds, and even a few flamingos. George's wife, Lois, loved colorful birds, so she made sure they surrounded her. (Courtesy Denise Sewell.)

Even in early 20th century, honey production was a significant industry in Wildomar. Boxcars full of honey left the area every year. Double-stacked hives are seen in this 1910 view of the Laguna Apiary owned by Rudolph Brown. Bees could be troublesome, as they established themselves into hollow spaces of olive, eucalyptus, and pepper trees and sometimes permanently inside homes. (Courtesy David A. Brown.)

Phil Mobley, a fourth-generation beekeeper, is looking over the construction of the honey processing plant in Wildomar in 1980. Phil and his wife, Katie, decided to settle down here, operate a local family business, and raise a family of their own. (Courtesy Phil Mobley.)

Sundance and Nishia wander over the freshly poured concrete on the site of the future honey factory. No fences are visible in the fields around the site. Until the early 1980s, nomadic sheepherders would bring their flocks to Wildomar and simply allow them to graze on any unfenced property. Both sides of Central Street and Baxter Road were occasionally blocked by flocks of sheep. (Courtesy Phil Mobley.)

This is a view overlooking the factory (center left) at the intersection of Central Street and Baxter Road in 1980. On a good day, the plant would process 8 to 11 drums of honey. Each 55-gallon drum weighed about 675 pounds and was shipped by truck to the Sue Bee plant in Anaheim on Highway 71, which ran nearby. The honey was blended to modify the crystallization rate on the shelf. (Courtesy Phil Mobley.)

The original processing plant (shown above in 1977) added a solar unit in 1984 to reduce dependence on electricity. The steel frame structure was operational until 1988 when it burned to the ground, only to be replaced with an almost identical facility. There are very few flowering plants in the October to February time frame, so the downtime was used to repair the equipment and maintain the hives. (Courtesy Phil Mobley.)

The Mobleys had to address the lack of hot water and electricity on the site. The invention of the unit shown here provided an alternate means to remove the comb. Rotating beater units ground the outside of the comb in lieu of the usual method of hot wire cutting. The arms projecting out the back allowed the units to be loaded and automatically processed. According to Plato, "Necessity is the mother of invention." (Courtesy Phil Mobley.)

To facilitate the loading and unloading of the beehives, a special cradle that rotated on a boom was made by Hopper Steel in Bakersfield. This allowed individual hives on uneven ground to be moved directly for transport. (Courtesy of Phil Mobley.)

The hives would be moved to the location of the flowering plants. In Riverside County, this included large citrus groves and the vegetation on the hills, especially buckwheat and black button sage. Beekeepers would follow the flowers, spending some time in central California where alfalfa and cotton were irrigated crops. The Mobleys processed all the honey at their facility in Wildomar. (Courtesy Phil Mobley.)

Pastor Bruce Goddard held the first services at Faith Baptist Church in 1982 at the DePasquale Hall on Catt Road (behind the U.S.A. gas station). By 1985, the church had grown, and this tent was needed for the services. The first of three tents over nine years, the church moved in 1997 to the old Inland Valley Hospital site. Today over 1,200 people attend Sunday services. (Courtesy Faith Baptist Church.)

This building at 32657 Central Street (at the corner of Front Street) was constructed with adobe bricks by Adelbert McKinney in 1930. He used a recipe from a department of agriculture pamphlet as a guide. The adobe bricks were cast on the property.

The Harold and Marian Smith home at the east side of I-15 and Baxter Road was constructed around 1950 out of cinder blocks and adobe. The adobe was cast on the property using a fire pit.

Located to the right of the mailboxes on a 40-acre parcel, the Quonset hut at 23551 Baxter Road was used as temporary living quarters during the building of the adjacent Skenfield house. The windmill supplied a trickle of water to the hut. One section of the house is adobe. In 2001 when this picture was taken, Baxter Road, located east of the freeway, was a dirt road. Rural mail delivery is still the order of the day, as evidenced by the mailboxes.

The Hillman ranch, the Kelley ranch, and the Leal ranch were all names for the same ranch at different times. The ranch was located near the present-day Anne Sullivan School. Termites had weakened the two-story Victorian style structure, which was taken down around 1970. The Hillman ranch consisted of a total of 72 acres. It was planted with dryland alfalfa.

Morris Brinkehoft, Leon Simmons, and Phil Baccus are relaxing in the kitchen of their adobe house. White paint on the walls was used to reduce the amount of internal lighting required. The adobe came from a factory in Escondido. There is no straw in the bricks. The building laws had just changed, and the bricks had to be coated with an emulsion made of cattle blood. (Courtesy Mary Diane Simmons.)

Norma, Hope, and Leon Simmons enjoy some time under the shade trees around the house. There was no electricity until the early 1960s. The water for the house came from a spring above the property and traveled by gravity flow into the house. (Courtesy Mary Diane Simmons.)

The Simmons family called their homestead "Road's End Ranch," as it was located at the end of Catt Road (now Smith Ranch Road). Unfortunately for history, the adobe structure burned to the ground in 1998. With the adobe bricks for walls, the fire burned hot as if in an oven, incinerating everything. (Courtesy Mary Diane Simmons.)

This pinto looks questioningly at the photographer. In the background, the log and mortar structure of the barn on Palomar Avenue a few houses past Gruwell Road.

Sydney and Julia Smith built this cabin at 25025 Catt Road. Built with native stone facing, it was taken down stone by stone and the stone was stored when it had to be dismantled to make way for a housing tract. (Courtesy Sydney Van Loon.)

The Smiths built a water storage reservoir with gravity delivery out of the natural springs from the hills. (Courtesy Sydney Van Loon.)

In some equestrian circles, one is never too young to learn to ride. Julie Smith demonstrates how it is done. (Courtesy Sydney Van Loon.)

In 1954, Wildomar had the excitement of an oil well being drilled. The drilling company acquired oil and mineral leases from the landowners and drilled a well on property just west of the Wildomar Cemetery. The well first hit "promising indications" (oil), then layers of hot and/or mineral water. It was judged that there was an insufficient quantity to pump. The well is still there, capped about 6 feet below the surface. (Courtesy Dave Turner.)

Five

THE CITY OF WILDOMAR

The level of community involvement in governance issues has been unusually strong in Wildomar. Throughout its history, individuals committed to their Wildomar have committed their lives and their money to better and preserve Wildomar. Almost out of nowhere, one community organization after another springs up having the whole interest of the community at heart. Some of these Wildomarians and organizations have been mentioned in this book. There was not enough room to include all of them.

The neighboring cities of Murrieta and Lake Elsinore made a number of attempts to split Wildomar and incorporate the portions that would be economically beneficial to them into their cities. Fortunately, Wildomar has had a strong sense of community and strong desire to continue its way of life. In 1990, Wildomar Incorporation Now (WIN) led the effort to make Wildomar a city and preserve it as a unique community. This was a grassroots effort that demonstrated Wildomar's spirit.

There were many obstacles, as both the State of California and the local LAFCO agency made the road to cityhood a strenuous and difficult journey. In February 2008, the issue finally went to a vote. The vote was in favor of incorporation. On July 1, 2008, the first city council was sworn in during a ceremony at Elsinore High School (located in Wildomar). Robert Cashman became the first mayor of Wildomar, Bridgette Moore the mayor pro tem. Marsha Swanson, Scott Farnam, and Sheryl Ade were the other council members in the first city council. Another chapter in the history of Wildomar is being written.

The Wildomar Interest League (WIL) was a nonprofit organization formed after the 1978 flooding to address issues including, but not limited to, flood control in Wildomar. The logo reflects the optimistic view of Wildomar's success and was designed by Marna O'Brien, a board member of the WIL. Once they were organized, the board tackled any and all Wildomar issues, interacting with the government and its agencies to solve the problem at hand.

In 1989, the Wildomar Municipal Advisory Council (Wildomar MAC) became the successor organization to the Wildomar Interest League. The council was an advisory board for the District 1 Riverside County supervisor. Members of the 2001 council consider an issue at a meeting in the community room of the library. Seated at the table from left to right are George Cambero, Pieter G. van de Bovenkamp, Melanie Wilson, Darrell Ruff, and Ron Kusayanagi. (Courtesy Jon Neal.)

Bob Buster, county supervisor for District 1 that includes Wildomar, addresses the MAC (seated on stage) and the residents of Wildomar on various community issues at the Wildomar yearly town hall meeting put on by the county. Attendance at these meetings was good.

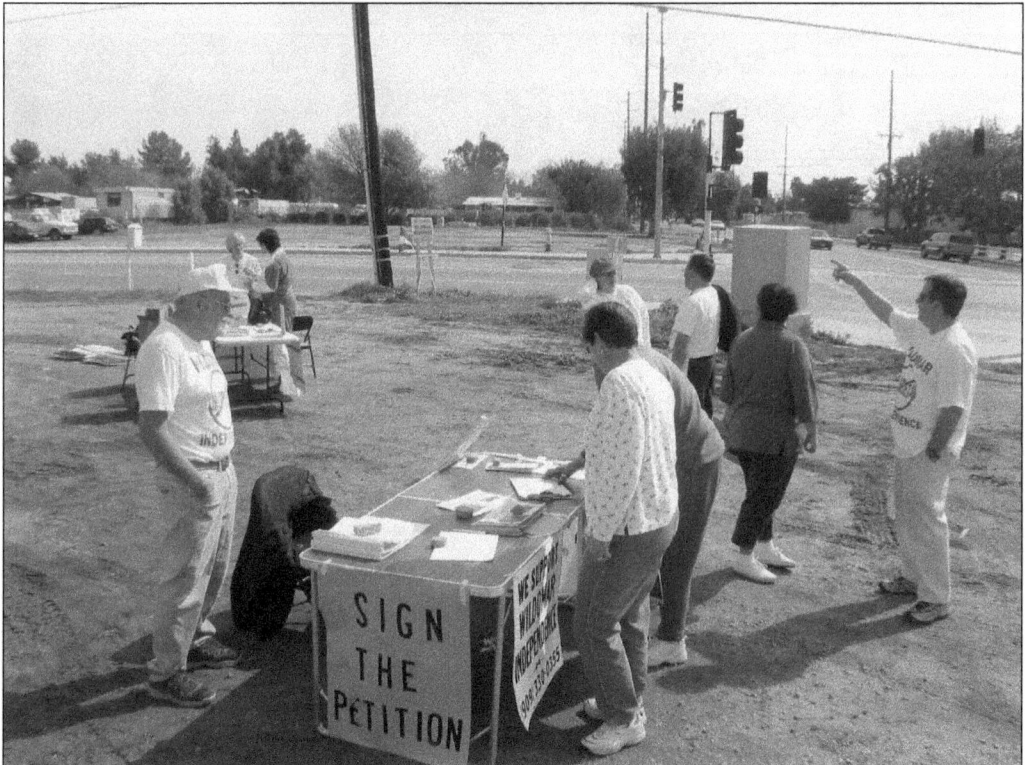

Incorporation was a grassroots effort organized under Wildomar Independence Now/Wildomar Incorporation Now (WIN). Jon Rodarme, Rick Estes, Sheryl Ade, and Gerry Stevenson talk to residents in a vacant dirt lot at the corner of Central and Palomar Streets in June 2004. The 2008 WIN members not shown above are George Cambero, Gina Castanon, Robert Cashman, Sharon Heil, Ed McOrmond, Kami Sabetzadeh, Stan Smith, and Tim Underdown. (Courtesy Jon Neal.)

Wildomar was under continual threats of annexation both by the city of Lake Elsinore and by the city of Murrieta. A group of Wildomar residents pray at the beginning of a city council meeting in Murrieta. Many are wearing T-shirts that read "Wildomar" along with a symbol indicating "no Murrieta." (Courtesy Jon Neal.)

Seated around the table at a WIN meeting at the Wildomar Senior Center in 2003 are, clockwise from the left front, Bob Cashman, Sheryl Ade, George Cambero, Paula Willette, Kami Sabetzadeh, Jon Rodarme, Bob Devine, Stan Smith, Bridgette Moore, Gina Castanon, Rick Estes, Gerry Stevenson, and Harv Dykstra. Members not shown are Ed McOrmond and Tim Underdown. The WIN committee met once a week for almost five years. (Courtesy Jon Neal.)

On November 9, 2008, 18 years after the first cityhood effort was started, the voters approved Proposition C (Wildomar incorporation) by 60 to 40 percent. The city officially started at an inauguration ceremony on July 1, 2008. At the conclusion of the event, fireworks lit the sky in celebration of our independence. Outside the new city hall in 2009, the Wildomar flag proudly waves in the wind. (Courtesy City of Wildomar.)

Visit us at
arcadiapublishing.com

······································